Social_Text_ **148**

Sexology and Its Afterlives
Edited by Joan Lubin and Jeanne Vaccaro

After Sexology · _Joan Lubin and Jeanne Vaccaro_   1

**Race and the Integrity of the Line: Sexology and Representations
of Pleasure** · _Amber Jamilla Musser_   17

**On Stalling and Turning: A Wayward Genealogy for a
Binary-Abolitionist Public Toilet Project** · _Susan Stryker_   37

Four Gestures toward a Trans-Mad Aesthetic of Space
Lucas Crawford   55

**Cripping the Welfare Queen: The Radical Potential
of Disability Politics** · _Jina B. Kim_   79

T0340618

After Sexology

Joan Lubin and Jeanne Vaccaro

Is sexology over? What does one do with its history, at once a seemingly remote relic and a persistent logic of biopolitics today? Sexology is both distant and persistent, signifying an outmoded pseudoscience at the same time that it underwrites the historical violences of racialization and underpins the long history of biopolitics that continues to exert a shaping force on the present. While sexology may seem like a digression from the mainstream of the history of science, and in some cases even from the mainstream of the history of sexuality, its discreditation is precisely the condition of possibility for its perdurance. "Sexology and Its Afterlives" begins from the premise that the history of sexology lives in the infrastructures of the present. Sexology's reorganization during the twentieth century has, in the contemporary moment, given it the force not so much of science as of policy, aesthetics, infrastructure, architecture, institutions, cultural production, and ideology. Foucauldian accounts of the modern subject have described the trajectory from *scientia sexualis* to contemporary biopower in terms of the encoding of sex into discourse. This special issue builds on this genealogical account by tracking the material consequences of that epistemic shift in sexual science. Locating the afterlives of sexology in material and aesthetic form, this issue engages the largely unmarked detritus of a disaggregated sexological project, whose components have found renewed life in the biopolitical apparatus.

We take the term *afterlife* to refer to the recrudescence of sexological aesthetics, modes, styles, and logics in the ongoing present. Rather than focusing on the historical alterity of sexology as social science, "Sexology and Its Afterlives" centers sexology as a field formation and knowledge project in its expansive form. Sexology is not just historical; its medium of cultural consequence is not just discursive, ideological, or otherwise linguistic; and its parameters are not just those of a science, strictly speak-

DOI 10.1215/01642472-9034376 © 2021 Duke University Press

ing. This special issue therefore invites engagements with sexology and its afterlives that include but also deliberately exceed the discursive, scientific, and historical aspects of the science of sex. Sexology was only ever partially institutionalized by that name. In the post-WWII period in the United States, many of the epistemologies, methods, practices—and along with them, many of the disciplinary functions and discriminatory logics—of sexology were thoroughly institutionalized under many other names: gender clinics, the welfare state, the "war on drugs," the prison-industrial complex, the criminalization of sex work, and many others. We hold these sites to collectively limn the afterlives of sexology that animate the present.

As we know from Foucault, *scientia sexualis* does not merely supersede *ars erotica* but, rather, rescripts its rituals and logics into a new program for systematizing social relations to sexuality.[1] Guided by this insight, this special issue excavates the persistent aesthetic logics underwriting the codification of sexological knowledge as it continues to structure the conditions of possibility for minoritarian survival. Centering an analysis of institutionalization through its spatial arrangements and material forms, rather than its signal genres like the case study or patient file, this issue turns to sexology not to recover or rehabilitate its violent history but to identify and activate the networks of coalitional actors, connected histories, and linked liberation struggles that have persisted alongside the atomizing and systematizing drives of sexual science. The contributors to this issue collate the aesthetics of the human sciences with their histories and politics by using methodologies from such fields as critical race studies, disability studies, literary studies, queer and transgender theory, psychoanalytic theory, feminist theory, visual culture, architecture, and design. This issue populates the sexological archive with an expansive array of examples that reflect its multifarious constitution and uneven diffusion: post-Katrina New Orleans, utopian psych wards, stand-up comedy, the mythology of the welfare queen, concentration camps, public toilets, gender dysphoria, Ulysses the glass dildo, and COVID-19.

By revisiting key texts, figures, and moments in the history of sexology and enlivening their analysis with attunement to the aesthetic, this issue forges interdisciplinary connections, linking divergent discourses of the politics of difference. "Sexology and Its Afterlives" brings together scholars working in various disciplinary and interdisciplinary frameworks, not to reconcile their disciplinary protocols but to exploit the discontinuity of those protocols as an opening onto the ruptural space of politics itself. In that way, it aims to maintain the space of discontinuity between disciplinary discourses in order to keep in view the complicated space of lived political action. While the contributions to this issue each attend to different aspects of the history of sexology, they all share a conviction that submitting its aesthetics to analysis and revision might extend our critique of its violent legacies and histories to prefigure another politic. The contributions to this issue show how sexology has dissimulated and disaggregated, finding new footings for its logics and tactics in the signal protocols of neoliberal management: urban planning, gentrification, universal design, public health, biometric surveillance, and the datafication of the human. The intellectual and activist project of dismantling the edifices of power demands contending with the ongoing legacies of sexological knowledge. Rather than subscribe to a programmatic method or topic, the contributions to this issue collectively inhabit its conjunction of terms to revise, renovate, and remodel the history of the human sciences as they ramify in the present.

Sexology has been a modality of state discipline and public hygiene projects, including eugenics, reproductive control, and biometric surveillance, and yet its consolidation as a scientific field has been idiosyncratic and haphazard. What has been—and what has become of—the referent of the term *sexology*? As much as sexology has been an effective instrument of the dispensation of state violence, its operations have been unevenly captured by models of power derived from theorizing highly systematized state repression projects. A knowledge project need not be coherent or hegemonic to be consequential, and in fact, as many of the contributions to this issue demonstrate, the incoherence of sexology was perhaps as effective in its introduction of damaging notions into the social field as its unified scientific perspective might have been. How might one relate to the incoherence of the sexological project without minimizing its violence? How might one acknowledge the only ever emergent and largely discredited work of sexology without amounting to an apologia for its profound utility as an instrument of discipline and oppression? Historically, sexology's low burden of proof has been in direct proportion to the utility of its truth claims for social control. What were the claims sexology made that it could not quite support, and how did it manage those margins of error and produce its truth effects?

Far from a systematized project, *sexology* was and is, as Janice M. Irvine wrote, "an umbrella term."[2] Writing in 1990, Irvine identified the consequences for contemporary sexual politics of a century-long crisis of authority in the professional discourse of sexology that reached fever pitch in the postwar United States. Irvine notes that

> even after a century of sexual science, sexology is relatively obscure as a profession and is as likely to evoke blank stares, or snickers, as nods of respectful recognition. . . . Yet thousands in this country count themselves as professional sexologists. They work as therapists, educators, researchers, or administrators in settings that range from universities and social service

agencies to religious institutions and private practice. Because of the multi-disciplinary nature of sexology, practitioners usually identify with another field of study, such as medicine or psychology.[3]

Irvine's study of postwar sexology makes clear not only the capaciousness of the discipline but also, more significantly, its infiltration of almost every branch of human sciences and social services. Sexology has been much more successful at generating mobile concepts and terms for uptake by other disciplines than it has at creating total theories of its own. This state of affairs can make it a strange object of study, as *sexology* names a diffuse discursive space that spans time periods, geographies, institutions, and social actors of many different kinds.

Most narrowly defined, *sexology* names the project of cultivating the health of bourgeois subjects—and that project has itself taken many forms. Grounded in the much longer history and violence of colonial contact, this project was formalized and perpetrated in nineteenth- and twentieth-century Europe and America by a group of white men, and a few white women, who were unevenly credentialed, primarily nonmedical professionals, academics, and reformers. This motley set of credentials characterizes not just the founding figures of the field, which one might necessarily expect not to have been credentialed in it; hardly any self-professed sexologist at any point in the field's history has been certified by that name. *Sexology* names not just a set of professional sexologists but a set of contingent knowledge practices, developed to allay historically specific manifestations of racial anxiety. The maintenance work required to sustain the fantasy of white supremacy has often been outsourced to sexology, which conscripts people—enslaved, coerced, and dispossessed—as experimental subjects whose bodies are compelled to testify to their alterity from the norm. Even as sexology attempted to draw a bright line between the normal and deviant, the healthy and the pathological, it ended up generating a cross-hatched grid of incoherence, incapable of stabilizing any one binary without tautological recourse to the others. The array of subject positions from which one might enter into the difference matrix of sexological knowledge thus also included bourgeois subjects seeking out a better fit for their own position of power, as well as minoritized subjects actively seeking subjection to science as a mode of recognition, redress, or simply relief.

Sexology is a science of the sexed human body, but that has only occasionally meant that it is a biological science. In the postwar United States it was fitfully institutionalized as a research science of human behavior, a laboratory science of endocrinology, a social science of public hygiene and criminology, and a clinical practice of gender diagnosis and treatment. Even when sexology has fixated on the human qua biological organism, it has appealed to social and material forms in excess of the sexed subject for explanation, control, and cure. As Greta LaFleur has shown, sexology was both "fundamentally a biopolitical science," operating on society at population scale, "and, just as importantly, it was also a field of study organized around the human body" and its anatomy, identifications, and desires.[4] As a science, sexology has admitted of multiple competing theories of its proper object, ranging from the organic to the psychological, environmental, mechanistically behavioral, and much else besides.

"Sexology and Its Afterlives" is interested in the remnants of diagnostic taxonomies that continue to organize and constrain lived experience. Sexology as a science has been multiply discredited without being wholly rejected, such that it was in a way never dismissed as much as dismantled and reconstituted in many guises, forms, and logics. Thus, this special issue is concerned with how that project has been concretized in material, architectural, and aesthetic forms that give it a solidity and duration that far outlive sexology as a scientific discourse. The contributors to this issue identify both familiar sites of sexological persistence (the sex-segregated public toilet) as well as less immediately obvious ones (the Moynihan report, redlining, the army base) as executing the unfinished business of the sexological project. Thinking across these sites, it becomes clear that sexology's fundamental protocol and primary legacy, its mode of operationalizing bodily difference as public policy and infrastructure, is segregation. Sexology mobilizes sex binarism as a fundamental mechanism of racialization, relentlessly policing the boundaries of the human with architectures and ideologies of partition. Public infrastructures of segregation proliferate policies and fantasies that become segregationist technologies of their own, underwriting ideologies of personal responsibility and individual autonomy that deny the reality of a shared ontology of interdependency. Focusing analysis on the design of sexology's afterlives underscores the enduring legacies of the sexological project that subtend the entanglements of race, sexuality, and bodily capacity with current regimes of classification and surveillance. Each of the contributors to the issue thus identifies historical anchors of sexological knowledge and violence and seizes on its unfinished business to nominate contemporary expressive registers (minority literary form, contemporary indigenous painting, embodied performance, pelicans in flight) that recapture some of the productive incoherence of sexology to open up rather than consolidate the matrix of difference and identity.

The contributions to this issue share a particular focus on the interlocking logics of the sciences of human difference in the United States, identifying a distinctive genealogy of contemporary neoliberalism as postwar sexological discourse cleaves away from its European precursors to abet the conglomeration of the university, clinic, state, and corporation. Sexology is a colonial science, and as the United States increasingly exerted its imperial force on the world stage after WWII, its deployments of sexological science became both more aggressive and more identical with statecraft as such, insidiously most violent where they are also least identifiable with the long history of sexological subjection. "Sexology and Its Afterlives" attempts to capture the undead quality of sexual science and its perpetual resurfacing around questions of power, embodiment, and the distribution of care, life, health, death, and risk. The consequences of sexual science on lived experience remain as real as ever, though they are less recognizable and more diffuse, called things like *biotech* and *national security*. If one sets out to study sexology by identifying people and things that announce themselves by that name, one will be missing out on most of the field, especially as one moves away historically and geographically from fin-de-siècle Europe.

Recent scholarship enlivened by this insight has moved to extend genealogies of sexology, locating its antecedents and identifying its nascent logics in times and places remote from nineteenth-century Europe, which its first wave of historians and critics identified as its defining locus.[5] This new wave of scholarship, which comes at the question of sexuality through postcolonial theory and transnational American studies, provincializes fin de siècle Europe and postwar America, rightly asserting that sexology is more temporally and spatially capacious than tight focus on those centers of activity would suggest.[6] The expansive remit of sexology reframed in this way requires pursuing its histories multiply and variously, from tracing its biopolitical imperatives to early American settler colonial genocide, dispossession, and enslavement to its colonial elaboration in the global South and the global "contact zones" of sexual science.[7] This issue builds on recent scholarship on sexology, empire, and racial formation; the history of sexuality and science in early America; and the history of deviance and intersectional liberation struggles.[8] As this range of scholarly approaches testifies, the disaggregation and diffusion of sexology over time, and the many different historical and local forms of appearance of sexual science, mean that studying it now is a genuinely interdisciplinary prospect. And it is not just interdisciplinary at the level of methods; it is also multimedia and multimodal—everything from contemporary literature to bathroom design bears the trace of a sexological impress. As the contributors to this issue show, sexology's afterlives manifest aesthetically in the line drawings of contemporary art, infrastructurally as racialized public health and housing crises, architecturally and institutionally as psych wards, and many other ways besides.

This issue understands the history of the sciences of sex, and the sexological project in particular, to be foundational to contemporary political struggle, making it a matter of renewed interest for queer studies, transgender theory, critical race theory, decolonial studies, mad studies, and disability studies. Sexology is implicated in all these fields in part because it operated on the premise that all forms of bodily and psychic difference index one another, consolidating a classificatory matrix that has since been disaggregated into divergent political programs and intellectual legacies. Thus, while sexology has a very different status in the history of each of these fields, this special issue is an attempt to enliven interdisciplinary conversation grounded in shared histories in order to transcend the immanent critique of field formation and articulate how sexological thinking organizes social life. The collected essays reveal that institutionalization not only is an ideological project but also entails epistemologically consequential spatial configuration, uncovering the construction project of the interdisciplines within which we are working.

"Sexology and Its Afterlives" interprets the sexological archive in an expanded field not to deconstruct it into a metaphorics that locate it anywhere and everywhere but, rather, to map its grammars in diffusion and multiply its genealogies. Our use of the term *afterlife* to describe the trajectory of sexology is meant to signal both how sexology continues to thrive in new forms and how its originary logics are reanimated and redoubled in newly configured segregationist technologies whenever the threat of collectivized difference looms too near. Sexology is both a densely historical phenomenon and a persistent contemporary presence, all around us as logic and form. To study the afterlives of sexology in both these senses, we turn to what Roderick A. Ferguson has called "pedagogies of minority difference" whose collective antecedent is sexology, even as their more proximate provenance is the Cold War.[9] We thus locate the coordinates of this special issue in terms of postwar histories of American imperialism, infrastructural elaboration, institution building, and foundation funding as much as in terms of histories of new social movements and identitarian theories and field formations. Building on the insights of Ferguson, Jodi Melamed, Robyn Wiegman, and others that locate minority field formations in the imperial logics of Cold War American statecraft, this issue stages a conversation among minoritarian field formations to consider how sexual science mediates, structures, organizes, and controls interactions between postwar institution building and postwar knowledge projects.[10]

Even as the dominant trajectory of the postwar era has been toward an ever increasing privatization of difference, identity was scarcely a foregone conclusion of sexology.[11] The most vital afterlife of sexology may in the end be that it has proliferated rather than consolidated theories and vocabularies for describing the relationships between and among sexuality, self, and embodiment. As much as sexology has underwritten the hegemony of identity as how we name embodied difference, it also generated a cacophonous array of terms and theories that have potentiated the critical insights of minority difference fields. To say that minority difference fields are "potentiated" by sexological excess is not to assert that they are determined by it. Sexology created more concepts than it could control, generating a sense of the problem space of embodied difference more than a definitive taxonomy. Critical theorists have found generative tools in the detritus of the sexological project to steer us toward richer notions of intersectionality and interdependency. In this issue, Amber Jamilla Musser reads the nominal universalism of sexological line drawing for its unwitting capacitation of Black "sensuousness"; Susan Stryker takes the multiply binaristic history of the bathroom as mandate for a "binary-abolitionist" project; Lucas Crawford reads the psych ward for a "trans-mad aesthetic of space"; and, in the issue's final essay, Jina B. Kim reads "minority literary forms" against the mythology of the welfare queen to arrive at what she calls "crip-of-color critique" grounded in a notion of shared dependency. Across the issue, newly imagined sites of collective politics come into view as a payoff for working through the stalled-out imaginaries of sexological binarisms.

"Sexology and Its Afterlives" pursues a genealogy of minority difference knowledges that alights upon sexology as epistemic antecedent and traces its diffusion into the institutional and epistemic architectures of interdisciplinary and coalitional scholarly praxis. In "Race and the Integrity of the Line: Sexology and Representations of Pleasure," Musser locates her engagement with sexology most proximately in her own embodiment of professional expertise, generating an autotheoretical investigation of racialized, feminized, queer inhabitations of the authority of sexual expertise. Her essay begins by zeroing in on the moment in the 1930s when line drawings were incorporated into sexological tracts in an attempt to vouchsafe their objectivity, demonstrating how aesthetic strategies aided and abetted the scientificity of sexology as it struggled to assert its distance from pornography. Musser's attention to line as the sine qua non of sexological objectivity reveals how an aesthetics of objectivity reverse-engineered respectability by centering, rather than repressing, graphic visual depictions. Attending to the lines of sexology's charts, graphs, diagrams, and anatomical illustrations, she finds surprising continuity between Robert Dickinson's line drawings of vulvas and William Masters and Virginia Johnson's line charts rendering the data on female sexual response: both are inscrutable, amounting finally to a visual expression of normative attachment rather than a data visualization.

Musser reads gynecological line drawings of genitalia as data portraits, conjuring a sexological subject by means of the representational strategies devised to depict her sex. She looks to the history of gynecology to theorize the formal techniques and aesthetic parameters for representing the raced and sexed subject of pleasure. Musser notes that anatomical illustrations, charts, diagrams, and case studies—the signal illustrative genres of sexology—entail different logics of scale and representativeness, each with their own relation to actual and idealized human bodies. She thinks across these divergences to specify the incoherence of race in the projects of Dickinson and Masters and Johnson, proposing that we might theorize race more broadly as a problem of scale. In the closing gesture of her essay, Musser meditates on the identity of the facial and the genital, scaling her inquiry to the "residue of racialization" that sexological representation labors to repress. Turning to a portrait of herself painted by queer Filipino artist Jevijoe Vitug, Musser shows how, in contrast to Dickinson, who uses the line to discipline female pleasure, Vitug uses zigzagging lines to capture the sensuousness and subjective pleasure of Musser's own racialized queer representability. Musser follows the line from segregation technology to technique of self-elaboration for the sensuous subject at work making sexual knowledge. Her essay reads the aesthetic history of sexology and the line in all its contortions to unseat the objectivity of the sexological project and reenvision its history as an interaction between aesthetic form and scientific tone. Locating the aesthetics of scientificity within the sexological archive creates a foothold to inhabit its history differently, not by reinhabiting its violent logics but by enlivening its unruly aesthetics.

We can see the lineaments of sexology in the present when we think about the sex segregation of bodies that labor, reproduce, eliminate, and are confined and subjected to violence. As the contributions to this issue show, to cobble together the credibility sexology secured for itself, it implicated a set of spatial grammars organizing relationships between people, things, places, and ideas. These grammars have consolidated into social scripts, mapping a topology of violence and risk for minoritized subjects that nominates sites like the bathroom and psych ward for intervention by public policy, legal, and activist efforts. As trans studies scholars Susan Stryker and Lucas Crawford each show in their respective contributions to this issue, assessing these familiar sites of social violence for their formal features, design elements, or aesthetic effects generates new accounts of their histories and functions, as well as new openings for activism and social justice. Historicizing the relationship between design and social engineering, Stryker and Crawford each consider the architectural management of the division between public and private and, by extension, those populations designated unfit for public life. Doing so affords them new insights about the history and consolidation of these spaces of risk, denaturalizing their institutional intractability and identification with violence. Their emphasis on the design principles of sex-segregated space allows a decoupling of proximity and violence, underwriting a broader understanding of the relational, rather than the agonistic, as the logic of public interaction. Both Stryker and Crawford identify how design can erect other conditions for social possibility among a public in formation—potentially even utopian ones.

In "On Stalling and Turning: A Wayward Genealogy for a Binary-Abolitionist Public Toilet Project," Stryker looks at the infrastructures erected on sexological premises, which have proved much more durable than the science itself. Her essay considers the gender-neutral public toilet project Stryker co-organizes with architect Joel Sanders. Galvanized by a renewed attention to the public bathroom instigated by transphobic violence and legislation, their gender-neutral bathroom is designed to be accessible, environmentally sustainable, and integrated into open spaces of transit, both indexing and generating a coalitional politics of public space. Stryker situates her collaborative project with Sanders in terms of a longer history of occupation and gentrification, centering the spectacular architectural forms that have most directly aided projects of social hygiene and the criminalization of the ill. She shows how the function of the toilet as a unit of social space has evolved over time, indexing the interlocking histories of sex work, racial segregation, gentrification, the criminalization of drug use and homelessness, disability, infrastructure, and transphobic violence. To the extent that the sex-segregated bathroom stall has been treated as a foregone conclusion, trans liberationist imaginaries are bound to stall out in it. Stryker seizes on this double sense of the stall as an occasion to work through the psychic impasses constraining trans experience.

Stryker takes up the bathroom stall not just as a site of inquiry and design but also as a formal mandate, composing her essay as a movement through a series of impasses where the path out is to break the binary. Stryker uses the public bathroom stall as an occasion to enact what she calls a "binary-abolitionist" project. By thinking trans in terms of the body as built environment, Stryker theorizes the mutual implication of racialized and gendered binaries in shaping social space. Centering the production of social relations through design, she adduces a rich history of the politics of the bathroom stall to consider both how this form has endured and to emphasize how it can be transformed to meet new needs in the present and future. Written as a series of meditations on stalling out, hitting psychic impasse, and reorienting, her essay proposes intervening on the ground beneath us, as a route to the processes within us, to transform our collective consciousness. Stryker's essay, and the toilet project it describes, is thus a powerful example of how an attention to design can transform what an emancipatory politics looks like: one form that trans affirmative action might take would be lobbying the international plumbing code to change their stipulation that the piping of all buildings be amenable to sex-segregated toilets. The plumbing, in fact, is also a theory problem. Radicalizing the adage "everybody poops," Stryker proposes the public bathroom as a commons. Recognizing the shaping force of architectural form, Stryker renovates the bathroom stall into the fundament of a new social configuration, enacting design initiatives underwritten by a deep investigation of the history and politics of partitioned space. Stryker takes it as a premise that social status does not precede the architectures of privacy and publicity, or the architectures of confinement and exposure, which is why she has undertaken to build new ones.

Working at the conjunction of trans studies and design theory, in "Four Gestures toward a Trans-Mad Aesthetics of Space," Lucas Crawford attends to the architectural forms that mediate the relation between bodily memory and historical trauma. One of the signal forms that mediate this relation has been the clinic. Following Foucault, Crawford notes the coconstitution of epistemologies of sex and madness and argues for a trans-mad analytic that is responsive to this common genealogy. He turns to the built environment of trans-mad administration to deepen the account of being subjected to expertise. Confronting the flatness of the clinical record, Crawford notes how it fails to capture the sensory surround of heteronormative clinical science. He draws on an autoethnographic analysis of his experience being hospitalized for the so-called pathology of gender dysphoria to investigate the speculative discourses of utopian design that conscript patients into envisioning their ideal rehabilitative environments. Wary of investing in the psych ward as a utopic space, Crawford's analysis guides him toward a critique of care that sees the pragmatic utility of semiprivate spaces of recuperation and self-consolidation.

Crawford deprioritizes the epistemologies of sexology in favor of its formal relations and aesthetic principles. He demonstrates that illness does not precede the spaces designed to house it, recognizing that mental illness is often a proxy for stigmatized modes of being, such as nonnormative gender identities, fatness, homelessness, addiction, and disability. He further notes that mental illness is always already architecturally constituted by the metaphorics of "stability," "breakdown," and "collapse." Crawford reads for the overlaps between social and spatial marginality, putting the art installation *Madlove: A Designer Asylum* by Hannah Hull and James Leadbitter in conversation with the performance art of Coral Short to highlight how contemporary cultural production can collectivize the experience of psychiatric isolation. Noting that "madness and transgender as epistemological and diagnostic categories . . . did not develop in cultural isolation," Crawford depathologizes gender not by sanitizing its associations with madness but by embracing a "trans/queer art of public emotion." Crawford identifies "embarking," "sensing," "emoting," and "collecting" as the features of what he calls a "trans-mad aesthetic," mounting a fourfold resistance to the spatial norms of mental health treatment: confinement, rationality, repression, and individualization. Crawford takes it for granted that the history of sexology is not worth rehabilitating, choosing instead to generate a poetics of architectural embodiment to foreground the imbrication of the body and institutional space. But there are many reasons beyond rehabilitation to contend with the enduring violences of the sexological project, not least to understand the present.

Stryker and Crawford, like Musser, both turn to the autobiographical to theorize the present and future of sexology. Even as autotheory is a genre with its own ambivalent take on agency, subjectivity, and positionality, these authors risk entertaining the sexological as a site of utopian fantasy and self-elaboration. Recognizing that sexology has always been characterized by its reliance on and appropriation of the experiential authority of its supposed subjects, autotheory short-circuits the extractive economy of embodied evidence to generate a critical opening. Sexology might have something to offer if we don't have to get stuck there. The bathroom stall can be a place one moves through, rather than a place where one stalls out. Both Stryker and Crawford think about these places of stagnation as spaces of transit—the most utopian psych ward, finally, is the one you can leave.

The collective inquiries that emerge across these essays prompt us to consider how the biographical exposes us to the complicated incoherences of the sexological project. Each of the contributors is attending to the afterlives of sexology, the epistemological and material forms it has set in motion that continue to animate the present—including the modern subject. Recognizing this footing puts us in the position of having to reconcile what it means to think oneself a subject of sexology. In the final essay of this issue, Jina B. Kim turns to one exemplary modern sexological subject to theorize its biography anew.

In "Cripping the Welfare Queen: The Radical Potential of Disability Politics," Kim traces the latent logics of the welfare queen out of the epistemological matrix of eugenic sex research and its racialized logics of dis/ability and dependency. She nominates the figure of the welfare queen to propose "crip-of-color critique," reading two works of contemporary "minority literary form"—Jesmyn Ward's *Salvage the Bones* and Sapphire's *Push*—for how they theorize "racialized regimes of disablement." Thinking at the intersection of race and disability, dependency emerges as a key term for Kim to foreground care, need, and access as vectors transversally organizing relations that identitarian vocabularies insufficiently capture. Dependency, she argues, is a shared condition and, as such, the grounds for a shared politic. As Kim argues, a simple inversion of the welfare queen mythology would emphasize autonomy and the accumulation of wealth as ideals. Instead, she turns to the literary, seeking imaginative ballast for a reorientation to the welfare queen as the exemplary figure to avow dependency as a shared, rather than exceptional or pathological, condition. In Ward's and Sapphire's texts she finds sociality configured around care rather than biology, enabling Kim to theorize race in terms of disability and failing infrastructure.

Kim activates disability as an analytic to detach it from the diagnostic apparatus, shifting the locus of disability away from individuals and into the social field that nominates some for systematic disablement. And yet she does this while taking up representations of disabled people. "To be clear," Kim states, "cripping does not necessitate looking for diagnostic evidence of disability in a text, nor does it prioritize the positive representation of identifiably disabled characters." This is not a contradiction; rather, it is a methodological avowal of the dialectic by which identity apprehends certain subjects and organizes the vocabularies by which they name themselves. This analytic strategy has pertinence for many identity-based fields, where the relationship between the identities that occasion the study and the methodological and analytical frameworks animated in their names has not always been straightforward. Activating a disability analytic to theorize race, Kim thinks across crip theory and women-of-color feminism. She genealogizes the mythology of the welfare queen, showing not only how race and dis/ability collectively constitute that mythic figure in the cultural imaginary but also that race and ability have a common genealogy as vocabularies for pathologizing and criminalizing dependency.

The contributors to "Sexology and Its Afterlives" are all working through one of the signal questions of minoritarian fields: what does coalitional politics look like as a methodology? The contributors collectively enable us to consider how intersectionality and interdisciplinarity comport with each other. Each is invested in the question of how identity structures the social world, but methodologically they begin their inquiries elsewhere. Kim, for example, taking dependency as premise, brings dynamism to the vocabulary of positionality by emphasizing connections between and among people who are presumed in advance not to be autonomous. Identity discourse emerges in this account as an effect rather than a cause. What would it mean to think intersectionality without identity? One approach has been exemplified by Jasbir Puar, who asks what it would mean to deconstruct identity without intersectionality—opting for a vocabulary of assemblage and arguing that intersectionality has been prone to freezing its subjects in "gridlock."[12] The contributions to this issue allow us to see yet another possibility, one in which experiential identity might be decoupled from identity as an analytic, enabling the latter to exert a critical capacity on the former.

"Sexology and Its Afterlives" reorients attention not just to the multiple histories of sexology but also to its multiple legacies still unfolding in the present. The genealogical work unfolding across this issue opens up a space to think about not just interdisciplinarity, identifying and pushing back against the ways disciplines have been siloed, but also the relations between and among minoritarian fields and their defining objects of analysis. The contributors call on disability studies, trans studies, Black studies, women-of-color feminism, visual culture, and the history of sexuality, generating emergent concepts, including crip-of-color critique (Kim), binary-abolitionist praxis (Stryker), a trans-mad aesthetic (Crawford), and a shift toward expressivity as a framework (Musser). The richness of these concepts is testament as much to the expansiveness of the sexological archive as to its ongoing and potential afterlives. When we think about the proper objects of sexology, we are not just talking about the distant past. We return to our opening question: what does one do with the history of sexology, at once remote and ongoing? Sexological authority is consolidated by a set of relays between the scientistic and aesthetic that are crystallized provisionally in material forms that give this dialectic duration and extension in time and space. The contributions to this issue draw on the history of sexology to draw out its aesthetics into a repertoire of unruliness. These strategies interrupt the segregationist logics that forcefully individuate subjects to contain their sociopolitical potential, suggesting that one of the afterlives of sexology might be collectivity.

Joan Lubin is a visiting scholar at the Society for the Humanities at Cornell University. Her research has appeared in *Post45*, *Women and Performance*, and *First Mondays*. She is currently completing a book project about mass cultural remediations of sexual science, tentatively titled *Pulp Sexology*.

Jeanne Vaccaro is a postdoctoral fellow at the ONE Archives and in the Department of Gender and Sexuality Studies at the University of Southern California. She is writing an aesthetic history of transgender as an identity category in formation, and her writing has been published in *TSQ*, *GLQ*, *Radical History Review*, among others.

Notes

1. Foucault, *History of Sexuality*, 70.
2. Irvine, *Disorders of Desire*, 1.
3. Irvine, *Disorders of Desire*, 2.
4. LaFleur, *Natural History of Sexuality*, 193.
5. Foundational accounts of the history of sexual and racial science by such scholars as Doan, *Fashioning Sapphism*; Irvine, *Disorders of Desire*; Meyerowitz, *How Sex Changed*; Escoffier, *American Homo*; Somerville, *Queering the Color Line*; Roberts, *Killing the Black Body*; and Terry, *American Obsession* have laid the groundwork for scholars to multiply the genealogies of sexuality and science.
6. See Arondekar, *For the Record*; Khana, *Dark Continents*; Chiang, *After Eunuchs*; Bauer, *Sexology and Translation*. See also the special issues LaFleur and

Schuller, "Origins of Biopolitics in the Americas"; and Schuller and Gill-Peterson, "The Biopolitics of Plasticity."

7. On the idea of the contact zone, see Pratt, "Arts of the Contact Zone."

8. There is an extensive and growing body of work in each of these areas. For a few exemplary works, see Chiang, *After Eunuchs*; Mitra, *Indian Sex Life*; Kunzel, *Criminal Intimacy*; Işıklar Koçak, "Pseudotranslations of Pseudo-scientific Sex Manuals in Turkey"; Rosenberg, *Confessions of the Fox*; Rosenberg "Molecularization"; Schuller, *Biopolitics of Feeling*; Kahan, *Book of Minor Perverts*; LaFleur, *Natural History of Sexuality*; Amin, "Trans★ Plasticity"; Doan, *Fashioning Sapphism*; Bauer, *Hirschfeld Archives*; Malatino, *Queer Embodiment*; Abdur-Rahman, *Against the Closet*; Heaney, *New Woman*; Terry, *American Obsession*; Love, "Doing Being Deviant"; Duggan, "Trials of Alice Mitchell"; Cohen, "Punks, Bulldaggers, and Welfare Queens"; and Rubin, "Studying Sexual Subcultures."

9. Ferguson, *Reorder of Things*.

10. See Wiegman, *Object Lessons*; and Melamed, *Represent and Destroy*.

11. LaFleur makes this case convincingly in the final chapter of *The Natural History of Sexuality*. Benjamin Kahan (*Book of Minor Perverts*) has also aerated the overdetermined identitarianism of sexuality by investigating the many competing etiological theories of sexual deviance.

12. Puar, *Terrorist Assemblages*.

References

Abdur-Rahman, Aliyyah. *Against the Closet: Black Political Longing and the Erotics of Race*. Durham, NC: Duke University Press, 2012.

Amin, Kadji. "Trans★ Plasticity and the Ontology of Race and Species." *Social Text*, no. 143 (2020): 49–71. doi.org/10.1215/01642472-8164740.

Arondekar, Anjali. *For the Record: On Sexuality and the Colonial Archive in India*. Durham, NC: Duke University Press, 2009.

Bauer, Heike. *The Hirschfeld Archives: Violence, Death, and Modern Queer Culture*. Philadelphia: Temple University Press, 2017.

Bauer, Heike. *Sexology and Translation: Cultural and Scientific Encounters across the Modern World*. Philadelphia: Temple University Press, 2015.

Chiang, Howard. *After Eunuchs: Science, Medicine, and the Transformation of Sex in Modern China*. New York: Columbia University Press, 2018.

Cohen, Cathy. "Punks, Bulldaggers, and Welfare Queens: The Radical Potential of Queer Politics?" *GLQ* 3, no. 4 (1997): 437–65. doi.org/10.1215/10642684-3-4 -437.

Doan, Laura. *Fashioning Sapphism: The Origins of a Modern English Lesbian Culture*. New York: Columbia University Press, 2001.

Duggan, Lisa. "The Trials of Alice Mitchell: Sensationalism, Sexology, and the Lesbian Subject in Turn-of-the-Century America." *Signs* 18, no. 4 (1993): 791–814.

Escoffier, Jeffrey. *American Homo: Community and Perversity*. Berkeley: University of California Press, 1998.

Ferguson, Roderick A. *The Reorder of Things: The University and Its Pedagogies of Minority Difference*. Minneapolis: University of Minnesota Press, 2012.

Foucault, Michel. *The History of Sexuality*, vol. 1. Translated by Robert Hurley. New York: Pantheon, 1978.

Heaney, Emma. *The New Woman: Literary Modernism, Queer Theory, and the Trans Feminine Allegory*. Evanston, IL: Northwestern University Press, 2017.

Irvine, Janice M. *Disorders of Desire: Sexuality and Gender in Modern American Sexology.* Philadelphia: Temple University Press, 2005.

Işıklar Koçak, Müge. "Pseudotranslations of Pseudo-scientific Sex Manuals in Turkey." In *Tradition, Tension, and Translation in Turkey,* edited by Şehnaz Tahir Gürçağlar, Saliha Paker, and John Milton, 199–218. Philadelphia: John Benjamins, 2015.

Kahan, Benjamin. *The Book of Minor Perverts: Sexology, Etiology, and the Emergences of Sexuality.* Chicago: University of Chicago Press, 2019.

Khana, Ranjanna. *Dark Continents: Psychoanalysis and Colonialism.* Durham, NC: Duke University Press, 2003.

Kunzel, Regina. *Criminal Intimacy: Prison and the Uneven History of Modern American Sexuality.* Chicago: University of Chicago Press, 2008.

LaFleur, Greta. *The Natural History of Sexuality in Early America.* Baltimore: Johns Hopkins University Press, 2018.

LaFleur, Greta, and Kyla Schuller, eds. "Origins of Biopolitics in the Americas." Special issue, *American Quarterly* 71, no. 3 (2019).

Love, Heather. "Doing Being Deviant: Deviance Studies, Description, and the Queer Ordinary." *differences* 26, no. 1 (2015): 74–95. doi.org/10.1215/10407391 -2880609.

Malatino, Hilary. *Queer Embodiment: Monstrosity, Medical Violence, and Intersex Experience.* Lincoln: University of Nebraska Press, 2019.

Melamed, Jodi. *Represent and Destroy: Rationalizing Violence in the New Racial Capitalism.* Minneapolis: University of Minnesota Press, 2011.

Meyerowitz, Joanne. *How Sex Changed: A History of Transsexuality in the United States.* Cambridge, MA: Harvard University Press, 2002.

Mitra, Durba. *Indian Sex Life: Sexuality and the Colonial Origins of Modern Social Thought.* Princeton, NJ: Princeton University Press, 2020.

Pratt, Mary Louise. "Arts of the Contact Zone." *Profession* (1991): 33–40.

Puar, Jasbir. *Terrorist Assemblages: Homonationalism in Queer Times.* Durham, NC: Duke University Press, 2007.

Roberts, Dorothy. *Killing the Black Body.* New York: Pantheon, 1997.

Rosenberg, Jordy. *Confessions of the Fox.* New York: Penguin Random House, 2019.

Rosenberg, Jordy. "The Molecularization of Sexuality: On Some Primitivisms of the Present." *Theory and Event* 17, no. 2 (2014). muse.jhu.edu/article/546470.

Rubin, Gayle. "Studying Sexual Subcultures: Excavating the Ethnography of Gay Communities in Urban North America." In *Deviations: A Gayle Rubin Reader,* 310–46. Durham, NC: Duke University Press, 2011.

Schuller, Kyla. *The Biopolitics of Feeling: Race, Sex, and Science in the Nineteenth Century.* Durham, NC: Duke University Press, 2018.

Schuller, Kyla, and Jules Gill-Peterson, eds. "The Biopolitics of Plasticity." Special issue, *Social Text,* no. 143 (2020).

Somerville, Siobhan. *Queering the Color Line: Race and the Invention of Homosexuality in American Culture.* Durham, NC: Duke University Press, 2000.

Terry, Jennifer. *An American Obsession: Science, Medicine, and Homosexuality in Modern Society.* Chicago: University of Chicago Press, 1999.

Wiegman, Robyn. *Object Lessons.* Durham, NC: Duke University Press, 2012.

Race and the Integrity of the Line

Sexology and Representations of Pleasure

Amber Jamilla Musser

In sexology the question of deviance is always nestled within that of plea-sure—pleasures reside within categorization, identification, pedagogy, and the acts or thoughts themselves. However, sexology's ideological investment in severing this connection produces a gulf between "normal" pleasure (often aspirational) and deviant behaviors (usually reduced to types). While the discourse of deviance prefers the detail, which charac-terizes the case study, as scientists seek to classify and specify difference, the norm, which is its other side, is often presented statistically through averages, numbers, and visually through the chart and diagram. Focusing on the line, this article traces the movement toward the precision promised by charts and diagrams within examinations of female pleasure, before culminating in the excesses of the zigzag.

Unpacking this centripetal force as it moves toward a representation of linear accuracy shows how norms were visually established in the early to mid-twentieth-century United States and how epistemological violence underlies the erasure of the "abnormal." Perhaps unsurprisingly, much of this excess, what we might think of as errant lines or blur, is racialized.[1] In this intertwining of race and representation, however, what emerges is not a fascination with the racialized sociological subject but, instead, a form of racialized compression that veers asymptotically toward erasure, pro-ducing racial residue and possibilities for resignification.[2] That the mat-ter of these aesthetic negotiations is sexual is not insignificant; it grants us another point of entry into thinking about the knot of representation, race, and sexuality where the history of spectacular, violated Black (or BIPOC) flesh hovers but is ultimately excised to maintain the desirability and (false) universality of the norm.[3]

Social Text 148 · Vol. 39, No. 3 · September 2021
DOI 10.1215/01642472-9034404   © 2021 Duke University Press

Sex and therefore sexology have been considered tools to understand not only the working of society writ large but also what underlies the very matter of the self. Indeed, the politics underlying the desire for a science of sex has historically been embedded in attempts to optimize pleasure to strengthen heterosexual marriages, which would presumptively align with a goal of fostering more robust nation-states and healthier populations. Female sexual happiness, in turn, is a crucial part of that equation because it is assumed to be the glue holding these marriages together.[4] Further, this emphasis on female pleasure is particularly focused on the idea of the female orgasm. To be sure, this taming of female pleasure into a graspable quantity—mysterious though it has remained—can also be registered as a fetishization of a moment of a lack of control in relation to femininity. That is, sexology's approach to the idea of the female orgasm is both an attempt to regularize it (and female pleasure) and a tacit acknowledgment that something uncontrollable remains. Here, we already hear an echo with the attempts to erase racialization's effects from the project of normalization and situate it within the realm of deviance. This produces an oscillation between the possibility of control through scientific means (notably in the service of helping men and nations) and a perpetual noncontrol. We can see this tension in a popular marriage manual's description of orgasm: "A sexual orgasm is a nervous spasm, or a series of pulsating nervous explosions which defy description. The action is entirely beyond the control of the will, when it finally arrives, and the sensation it produces is delectable beyond telling."[5] Despite this, attempts to figure out what orgasm was and how it could be induced remained a central part of sexological discourse.

Annamarie Jagose names this contradictory assemblage the "twentieth century orgasm," and her book *Orgasmology* is dedicated to making meaning from some of its contradictions. This entity, Jagose argues,

> is biological and cultural, representable and unrepresentable, as well as personal and impersonal, it is also and at once worldly and out of this world. . . . : twentieth-century orgasm is also innate and acquired; voluntary and involuntary; mechanistic and psychological; literal and figurative; trivial and precious; social and asocial; modern and postmodern; liberating and regulatory; an index for autonomy and self-actualization as well as for interpersonal and communal attachment; the epitome and the extinction of erotic pleasure; and indifferent and intrinsic to taxonomic categories of sexual difference and sexual orientation. These oppositions are not entirely specific to orgasm or without precedent: they draw their contradictory charge from the historic processes whereby sexuality has come to constitute a framework of intelligibility for sex.[6]

In identifying orgasm's relationship with sexuality, Jagose also points us toward the particular relationship among sexology, heterosexuality, and orgasm: "The utility of heteronormativity is not that it functions as a kind of ahistorical one-size-fits-all descriptor for relations between the sexes, but that it indexes the emergence of heterosexuality as a category internal to the normalizing protocols of the modern disciplinary system of sexuality itself."[7] In representational terms, this means that focusing on female orgasm as the signal of female pleasure allowed for a false equivalence between it and ejaculation, which sexology took as the most important aspect of male pleasure because of its correlation with procreation. This presumed correspondence led to efforts to discern reproductive purpose for female pleasure (a conundrum that continues to have abysmal political effects in relation to reproduction and rape) in addition to attempts to suture it to the same logic of the visible ejaculation—though only ever fitfully, as Linda Williams has famously described with respect to the particular tension between the idea of female orgasm and its representation in pornography.[8]

We arrive at the question of how to represent female orgasm with several challenges, the first being definitional (what actually constitutes orgasm?) and the second, a related quandary: what, then, constitutes visual evidence? Making orgasm visible entails making orgasm into a tangible event in which psychic changes, since they cannot be mapped in an "objective" scientific manner, are grafted onto physiological symptoms to become more easily readable. Robert Latou Dickinson, an illustrator and gynecologist, created innovative drawings of human sexual response in the early twentieth century, but he admitted gaps in his knowledge, particularly with regard to female orgasm. By 1966, however, William Masters and Virginia Johnson's *Human Sexual Response* claimed mastery over the physiology of orgasm.

In many ways both research projects overlap significantly. Their mutual desire to preserve the fabric of the (white) American family led them (via the logic of eugenics) to sex and the female orgasm. Unlocking the physiological and anatomical secrets behind orgasm was thought to provide the tools necessary for societal social engineering. In addition, both Dickinson and Masters had been practicing gynecologists before dedicating themselves to sex research: their attention to precise detail offers testament to years of medical practice, while their continued insistence on the nonerotic (scientific) nature of their work illustrates the pains taken to maintain a veneer of scientific integrity and professionalism. Beyond empiricism, both projects are unique in their attempts to represent the orgasm visually.[9] Though their methodologies differed—Dickinson preferred illustrations of normal orgasms (in specific women), while Masters and Johnson used photographs, diagrams, and charts to model a typical orgasm (belonging to a generalized "woman")—both attempted to capture movement and emotion in two dimensions. These are questions not just about science but about race and the politics of representation.

Anatomical Expertise and the Pleasures of the Line

Robert Latou Dickinson believed that many problems, including insomnia and menstrual pain, had their root in genital anatomy. To keep a record of his gynecological patients' current and potential difficulties, he made sketches of their uteri, cervixes, and vulvae, which he kept updated throughout their time with him. In 1932, the first edition of his *Atlas of Human Sex Anatomy* was published; it was a large compendium of his clinical illustrations of anatomical and physiological abnormalities alongside written descriptions of these case studies. The purpose of Dickinson's atlas is twofold: it is meant to serve a pedagogical function—the demystification of sex—while simultaneously distancing his research from pornography. This wielding of the illustrator's pen was in part a reaction against tactics of marriage manuals, which sought to titillate their readers with graphic descriptions, but the stated goal—to provide information that could help better marriages—was the same.

In the preface, Dickinson makes explicit the objectivity that underlies his pared-down lines and attachment to the norm: "Our protests against the sensual detail and the exaggerations and credulities of pornographic pseudo-science lose force unless we ourselves issue succinct statistics and physiological summaries of what we find to be average and believe to be normal, and unless we offer in place of the prolix mush of much sex teaching the simple statements called for in any sane instruction."[10] In Dickinson's argument for the pedagogical import of illustrating genitalia, we also find a critique of excess detail, which he calls sensual, that characterizes the literary.[11] This means eschewing realism in the drawings—despite Dickinson's work elsewhere producing realistic three-dimensional anatomical models—favoring instead schematic line drawings. He explains his choice: "By avoidance of realism in the illustrations, by minimal graphic statement, and diagrammatic representation wherever possible, it was thought that the erotic suggestiveness could be largely eliminated."[12] The moral and scientific arguments against sensuality, both visual and literary, are critical to Dickinson's attempts to assert himself as a legitimate researcher.

Dickinson used three different types of illustrations to make his arguments about sex. The first type demonstrates the quantity of observations made; most often these are drawings in profile, meant to suggest both a norm among his patients and the extent of their variation. Through these illustrations, Dickinson is teaching us about the value of the norm—he is showing readers the breadth that it can encompass and making an argument for the utility of a schema based on it. The second type of illustration comprises specific examples of various portions of the body; these offer evidence of Dickinson's ability to make specific, detailed observations. Both of these types of illustrations gesture toward Dickinson's professional authority by signaling his breadth of experience and observational expertise.

The third type of illustration, however, relies on the viewer's trust in Dickinson's knowledge; they are diagrammatic presentations of his hypotheses regarding sexual response. These schematic drawings are unfalsifiable because Dickinson acknowledges that he did not have access to what happens physiologically during intercourse—he was not a witness and could only speculate. His hypotheses were born from his use of wax cylinders and glass phalluses with subjects to visualize their sexual response. He relied on these instruments to measure both specific details and general changes that he observed: the wax allowed him to visualize the muscular workings of the vagina, which in turn allowed him to model vaginal movement during penetration and birth, while the glass phallus provided a way for him to exert force on the vagina so he could observe (by looking through it) how other internal organs respond to penetration. It is important to note that he treats these sessions not as simulated sex but, rather, as methods of providing an approximation of vaginal penetration. From these experiments, he creates a multitude of illustrations of different sexual positions, two of which explicitly treat orgasm.

In both illustrations we see Dickinson's attachment to the norm working in peculiar ways. While he does not attempt to describe a norm for all orgasms, he does use the idea of the norm to describe the response of two patients. The illustrations, then, are specific to individuals but do not indicate any one particular incident of orgasm. The threat of titillation is mitigated by these illustrations' relationship to the accumulation of knowledge. The first, figure 147, is Dickinson's attempt to illustrate the varied sexual responses that correspond to different positions—"woman above," "woman below," and "woman beneath his body high up on hers." The illustrations show a series of numbered curved lines, meant to show the range of clitoral movement, against the outline of a penis with an arrow meant to show the direction of penile movement. Here, Dickinson is using anatomical illustration to teach readers that "male induces maximum vulval responses by providing fullest clitoris excursion (and pressure desired)." The second illustration, figure 158, focuses more explicitly on the particularities of what happens during orgasm. It is culled from Dickinson's patient files and includes a brief case history in addition to many illustrations from different stages of the subject's life. Again, the woman's internal structures are defined against the outline of the glass phallus, whose measurements are given. Dickinson describes the movement of the uterus and clitoris during orgasm and notes the measurements of the woman's posterior and anterior vaginal wall. He also notes the patient's behavior during orgasm: "Orgasms vaginal and/or vulvar:

no levation grasp or throb; moaning, gasping, often powerful thrashing"; her favorite posture (woman on top) "explains the length of anterior wall of vagina." A biographical sketch of the woman is provided, along with confirmation of her facility for orgasm with her husband, a matter that Dickinson confirms with his visual analysis: "Vagina and quick vulvar color suggest [subject's] history."

Even as Dickinson searches for a visible marker of orgasm, his illustrations make clear that, beyond what he considers individual variation, he has been able to discern only patterns and postures of stimulation. Dickinson freely admits the difficulty of describing the orgasm: "If this is typical orgasm, then orgasms have not occurred more than a half dozen times in many millions of office examinations nor have they been noted in their wives by doctors familiar with the cervix, or else physicians have consistently hidden knowledge of such action."[13] Furthermore, female sexuality is considered only against penile activity. Even as Dickinson notes the importance of clitoral stimulation to orgasm, his techniques of visualization show that he understands female sexual response as intricately linked to penetration. In the absence of Dickinson's ability to describe a norm of sexual response, his illustrations display his notion that the sources and manner of stimulation are more important and more relevant than what exactly happens during orgasm. His emphasis on the intersubjective aspect of orgasm is reflected in how he presents his patient's description of her own sexual response:

> Married at 20, he partly impotent, she unawakened. Two children: widow. Second marriage at 26. He a reservatist statistician good for intromission an hour and 100–120 vigorous thrusts in succession, by count. Her crescendo was from breast to vulvar caress and increasing vigor of orgasm. As height close to the preceding, each 20, 24, 27, up to maxima of 40, 56, 63, 65 even 83 seconds: 7 or 8 in 205 seconds; 30 in half hour at times, 5 to 10 in sequence for a month at rates of 2, 3 times a day. No exhaustion, alert.[14]

Though her response is shaped in large part by the questions he asks her, the emphasis is on what her husband did to induce response rather than on her actual response. Though Dickinson is describing a female orgasm, his focus on context (marriage) and intersubjectivity (the orgasm could not take place without a partner) is more aligned with an investment in masculine agency. The intended pedagogical audience here is male.

This emphasis on what men can do to induce orgasm in their wives is not just reflective of the heteronormative ideology of early twentieth-century sexology; it also carries implications for thinking about race by invoking particular prescriptive norms around white femininity. Dickinson's invocation of a feminine passive receptivity centers on impressibility, which Kyla Schuller describes as "the capacity of a substance to receive impressions from external objects that thereby change its characteristics."[15] The concept of impressibility allows us to tangibly grasp the multiple levels on which these discourses of pedagogy function within sexology. The sexological reader, after all, must be sensitive to the surrounding world and able to incorporate its subtleties into sexual performances to maximize marital happiness. In these texts, this capacity for learning is the precondition for being able to attain the norm. This capacity is, however, profoundly racialized. In emphasizing learned responsiveness, Dickinson has implicitly centered white femininity while moving other forms of perceived response, which might be racially coded as more active or less reactive, outside the norm.

This logic extends to anatomy as well. Although the texts are geared toward teaching male partners how to induce orgasm, it is white women's bodies that have a particular responsiveness toward appropriate vaginal stimulation. Schuller examines this argument, in a more extreme form, as it plays out in the work of Elizabeth Blackwell and Mary Walker, two of the first female physicians in the United States. There, Schuller uncovers a reading of the vagina as "a crucial neurological structure."[16] In their arguments for racialized difference, Blackwell and Walker "extended the logic of binary sexual differentiation to incarnate the racialized capacity of openness and responsiveness in the vagina of the white woman."[17] Importantly, this openness "afforded white women greater capacities of stimulation and therefore development in both body and brain than their male counterparts or the sexually undifferentiated primitive."[18] Schuller's analysis reminds us that receptivity is not a race-neutral concept but something that is part of a set of hierarchized relations of gender, race, and sexuality.

Reading Dickinson's focus on modes of stimulation rather than female response in conjunction with Schuller's reminder that female vaginal responsiveness was racialized allows us to see why Dickinson did not dwell on female response. It was unremarkable, a racialized given, as long as white men learned appropriate modes of stimulation. Importantly, this complex system of racialized bias was transmitted through the mechanism of the line. Although the schematic line drawings do away with the threat of sensuality, this amorphous quality of sensuality is also where fleshiness or any quality of difference lies. This excision of difference manifests in several ways. First, there are Dickinson's explicit ways of excluding racial difference from his work in his atlas. In the entire compendium, there are two drawings of Black women—neither of which is credited to Dickinson. One, attributed to a French source, shows the position of the vulva relative to the chair while seated. Blackness is indicated not only in the caption, which is in French, but also by the shading of the skin with cross-hatching. The other drawing is of labia majora, described as a "Negress specimen from the Surgeon General's Museum published by Dr. Lamb." In this way Dickinson makes it clear that these are not data points that he consulted for his production of the sexological norms that emerge from his clinical work. Within the *Atlas of Human Sex Anatomy*, Dickinson included his composite of averages as drawings of "Norma" and "Norm-man." These measurements and the resultant figures, later transformed into white alabaster statues, were described as versions of "normal" Americans. This assertion of continuity between average measurements and normative behavior illuminates the multiple axes on which sexological representation operates. In this tautological structure, Dickinson gathers physiological data from white subjects and creates a "national" average, which becomes a way to divide normative and deviant people. Anna G. Creadick describes the movement between the representational and behavioral as endemic to this prewar moment: "Journalists and scientists regularly anthropomorphized the plaster figures, moving beyond their surfaces to hypothesize about their interiors. Such slippage from bodies to minds was not surprising; inquiry into the 'normal' American character was another significant academic project of the interwar and early postwar years."[19] That freedom from the pollution of eroticism and pornography manifests through a line that excludes blackness is an important reminder of how racialization enacts pressures on representation even and especially through its exclusion.

Triumph of Physiology and the Opacity of the Diagram

In contrast to Dickinson's hand-drawn illustrations, William Masters and Virginia Johnson used the diagram to present their information about orgasm. This layer of abstraction transformed physiological data into a combination of prose and lines that were tethered not to the anatomy of intercourse (as was the case with Dickinson) but to an argument about the physiology of response itself, an argument that, importantly, did not differentiate between sources or types of stimulation but instead posited a universal form of female response.[20] Race here is elided in different ways. Though Masters and Johnson did include some people of color in their analysis, their emphasis on the universality of physiology is emblematic of a logic of colorblindness and shift toward statistical thinking.[21] Here, the line severs the possibility of a racial analysis in part because it emphasizes the responses of particular organs rather than any individual's entire response, but this in turn leads to the questions of what kind of structure race is and how it manifests through representation.

Masters and Johnson's research presents a quantitative/numerical rendering of the orgasm, alongside a photographic/diagrammatic depiction and a qualitative/narrative representation. Like Dickinson, Masters and Johnson strove to achieve an aura of scientific objectivity to lend their project legitimacy. To this end, they used a vast array of technologies to collect the desired data on sexual response. They used multiple recording techniques, including film and photography, and their subjects (members of the academic community of Washington University in St. Louis) were asked to make multiple visits to their research laboratories. Generally, the subjects, who were predominately female, were taken to a room equipped with film cameras and told to engage with a thrusting machine, the technologically enhanced dildo Ulysses. This machine, calibrated to record measurements at various times during the encounter, provided penetration and could be adjusted for both speed and strength. The thrusting machine also had photographic capabilities so that various theorized stages of orgasm (excitement, plateau, orgasm, and resolution) could be mapped onto specific physiological moments. In subsequent interviews with the women, their recounted experiences were mapped onto Ulysses's data.

Human Sexual Response, the first book published from this research in 1966, is a combination of dense prose, diagrams, charts, and photographs, each geared toward the representation of orgasm. While the text dwells on details the images cannot capture, such as color variation, texture, smell, and sound, the images attempt to present a dynamic process. The images work to capture a body, but more precisely organs, in action. Though Masters and Johnson's research techniques involve analyzing the whole body's response to sexual stimuli, their presentation of the data takes each organ in turn, moving from external female genitalia to the clitoris, then the vagina, and finally the uterus. This process of internalization locates the orgasm simultaneously inside, outside, and on the body. As the scope of investigation moves inward, Masters and Johnson provide more diagrams to make these internal processes visible. This prioritizing of visual evidence, garnered through Ulysses's mechanical, "neutral" mediation, is meant to signal objectivity, while other ways of experiencing and documenting orgasm are seen as subjective.

The most important thing that Masters and Johnson's visuals convey is the idea that organs move during orgasm. The chart was one of their favored techniques for representing this dynamism, among them, an electrocardiogram of a female subject throughout sexual response, with the orgasmic time frame noted on the chart; a reading of orgasmic platform contractions against heart rate for the same time; and an intrauterine electrode measuring uterine contractions in orgasm against normal uterine irritability. Though Masters and Johnson attempted to provide a frame of reference for each chart, extracting useful information from them is challenging. The veneer of precision reveals only the fact of organ movement. The charts affirm the existence of a physiological change around what one terms *orgasm*, thereby establishing the utility of instruments, and not experience, for discerning orgasm.

Unlike the charts, which show the importance of data, the task of the diagram is to remap this information back onto the body. Masters and Johnson, in particular, use these schematic anatomical drawings to show readers where to locate orgasm on an abstracted body. Diagrams of the breast, clitoris, vaginal barrel (multiparous and nulliparous, surgically and nonsurgically constructed), female pelvis, and uterine elevation are shown during preexcitement, excitement, plateau, orgasmic, and resolution stages. These drawings are often accompanied by text describing physical transformations and by arrows indicating direction of the body parts' movements. On the one hand, their existence as a series points to an attempt to isolate movement. On the other hand, how this movement is represented makes it appear as though the body passes through a series of ideal "poses," the fluidity of its motion disturbed. The imposition of stages onto sexual response creates a clash between precision, which Masters and Johnson strive to achieve through their detailed anatomical renderings, and the temporal imprecision created by the fluid nature of movement. Effectively, the drawings represent nothing: they cannot capture the dynamic aspect of sexual response because they are limited by their static nature and their limited scale.

Masters and Johnson's reliance on measurement and statistics to create the fact of orgasm is testament to the power numbers possess to legitimate information. This tactic was common among several American sexologists; in addition to Dickinson and Masters and Johnson, Alfred Kinsey also famously favored numerical data. In part, we can attribute this use of evidence to the rise of statistics in the twentieth century. As Alain Desrosières argues, statistics allowed social scientists to "transcend individual or conjugal *contingencies* and to construct *more general things* that characterize for example the social group (for the sociologist) or the long term (for the historian or the economist)."[22] The loss of individuality in quantification is a double-edged sword: "On the one hand, it constitutes an 'obligatory passage point' . . . and is of extreme social import, but on the other hand it is implicitly considered to overlook the essential, to be impoverished, simplificatory and to explain nothing."[23] Eliminating the individual forges a sense of equality since the idea of the universal makes everyone equivalent (i.e., interchangeable) but simultaneously unable to actually embody the norm, which has become its own ideal. One manifestation of this impossible embodiment can be seen in Masters and Johnson's refusal to show the images that were actually taken by Ulysses or images of the setup required for their data retrieval—photographs or drawings of couples or individuals masturbating. These images, which provided Masters and Johnson with a more holistic image of sexual response, are exempted from public view. While we might argue that this has to do with a possible kinship to pornography, this omission reinforces the scientific status of the research. While their data is public, it is almost inscrutable—it is difficult for someone who is not an expert to understand what exactly is going on. Rather than employ visuality as a method of clarification, it becomes a tool of mystification. The body and its workings become vexing puzzles, better left to the domain of others to describe.

Complicating this representational terrain is the argument that the emergence of the statistical fact and removal of the individual have facilitated the conceptualization of a new type of subjectivity, what Gilles Deleuze terms the *dividual*.[24] While the emergence of sexuality as an entity to examine through sexology enables the construction of certain individuals such as the homosexual, the pervert, and so forth, statistical models of subjectivity rely on eradication of the individual in favor of a virtual figure who is impossible to actually materialize. The intersection of these ideas within *Human Sexual Response* produces a complex image of sexuality. It is divorced from aim and object, which locate sexuality within the subject, but at the same time this sexuality is held to be universal, a physiological response, and a statistical invention of mythic proportions. Masters and Johnson portray orgasm as a social fact held together by statistics and family therapy. Individual variation ceases to matter; what is important is the fact of orgasm. Its achievement is the most relevant piece of data; its nonachievement is the risk to be managed. This shift away from the individual (and the case study) toward organs and statistics is embodied through the aesthetics of the line. Masters and Johnson's diagrams and charts produce an affect of clarity even as they do not index anything in particular.

How, then, does race circulate in this system, and what does this tell us about what kind of entity it is? Masters and Johnson have made an argument that physiological response is the most important factor in theorizing sexual response while also rendering the actual matter of bodies opaque. Here, their use of the line severs sexual response not only from the whole individual but also from the sociological, which is one arena where Dickinson might argue the residue of difference lies. In making an argument that organs are the only thing that one should attend to, Masters and Johnson make it impossible to think with the larger landscape of sexual response where frameworks of intimacy and history might reveal themselves. As Janice Irving wrote, "They go one step beyond Kinsey, who based his notion of 'naturalness' on what people did, in that they base their idea of 'naturalness' on the physiological responses people exhibit."[25] Since Masters and Johnson's emphasis on physiology served the dual purpose of making their data appear both objective and the only observation worth noting, to imagine that race is physiological is to risk collusion with racist myths, but to imagine that it does not matter produces its own form of violence. In this schema, inclusion is not the question; instead, race hovers as a problem of scale. The precision of Masters and Johnson's lines, which abstract bodies but cannot represent particularities, cannot be thought in relation to the two scales: the metascale (sociological) and the individual, through which race matters.

Blackness and the Sexological Project

> The close-up of a face is as obscene as a sexual organ seen from up close. It *is* a sexual organ. The promiscuity of the detail. . . . takes on a sexual value.
> —Jean Baudrillard, *The Ecstasy of Communication*

The suturing of selfhood and sexuality goes beyond Jean Baudrillard's quick observation relating the face to genitals. It is the logic that underlies the construction of sexuality itself, as part of a transition toward linking sexuality with the unconscious in ways that both include and exceed genitalia.[26] I bring Baudrillard, theorist of spectacle, into the conversation here because his observation connecting the face and genitals enables us to more fully comprehend the working of sexology as a type of dual portrait. The interchangeability of faciality and genitality becomes indicative of sexologists' attempts to abstract sexualities (and subjectivities) into describable essences while also speaking to sexology's sociological and scientific functions. As scientific discourse, it is intended to portray either idealized or demonized sexual behavior, but it also inadvertently reveals much about the social and cultural mores of its practitioners and their milieu. The production of sexological discourse, then, traffics in multiple versions of the self: that which is idealized and that which lurks in shadows. In asking us to look for the set of relations (the promiscuity) to which the detail attaches, Baudrillard invites us to think robustly with the multitude of twentieth- and twenty-first-century possibilities of representation that emerge through the dividual: What happens when pleasure and selfhood bypass the genitals? Where can the residue of racialization find release?

This is to say, there are other ways to use the line that do not produce racialized exclusions. Here, I turn toward a portrait of me painted by Jevijoe Vitug, a contemporary Filipino American artist working in Queens (fig. 1). Like Masters and Johnson, Vitug works from photographs, but he uses abstraction to illuminate what the "objective" might miss. These lines do not offer racialization as a project of cross-hatched marks, nor are they part of a project to extract physiological data under the guise of precision. Instead, Vitug plays with the form of the line, using thick zigzags to compose the image. Unlike the lines produced by Dickinson and by Masters and Johnson, Vitug's lines are not seeking to excise race through (or in favor

Figure 1. Portrait of the author, by Jevijoe Vitug. Photograph by the author.

of) scientific rationalism; instead, they are markings from his indigenous Filipino heritage. He uses them to bring racialization explicitly into the grounds of representation. Here, the lines' thicknesses and curves convey opacity, not clarity. This foregrounding of the racialization of the lines highlights the amorphous representational space in which race circulates—it is present, but not reducible to identity (of either artist or sitter).[27] Instead, we can register racializing circulating as a theory of expressivity—both Vitug's and my own.

We might especially think with Jean Luc Nancy's meditation on the pleasure of drawing and the politics of representation. For Nancy, drawing is related both to the act, insofar as it involves an extension of self, and the result, which operates as its own enclosed form: "One draws—one traces or extracts—in order to show. One shows by extending or spreading out in front of oneself. Better, in order to show something well, in order to render it fully manifest, one must not cease drawing (if only to draw attention), and in order to draw out (trace or pull), one must not lose sight of the invisible extremity of the mark, the point by which the line advances and loses itself in its own desire."[28] For Nancy, drawing is not about mimesis but is instead a process of interpretation that reveals a form with its own representational logic (what we might call desires): "Drawing is therefore the Idea—it is the true form of the thing. Or more exactly, it is the gesture that proceeds from the desire to show this form and to trace it so as to show the form—but not to trace it in order to reveal it as a form already received."[29] In his deliberate separation between process and product, we find the space between representation and the object that sexological diagrams and charts want to collapse but that Vitug's painting allows to breathe. That space is what acknowledges both my and Vitug's racialization but does not demand that they become interchangeable. Instead, there is an ethical negotiation between them. Vitug's employment of Filipino zigzag lines signifies his attachment not only to his Filipino heritage but also to its unique representational system, which manifest in his use of symbols within the zigzag, spatial orientations, and pressure on the canvas. I do not have access to all of the ways that the painting signifies, but as Nancy suggests, the portrait is not an attempt to contain—it exists as its own form, distinct from that which it represents.

In this context, the zigzag might register as emblematic of the freedom of the line and the unruliness that Vitug permits. It offers a form of extension that is about not capturing the subject but expressing his own relationship to the concept of representation. Vitug's painted lines are echoes of those tattooed on him by Whang-od, the oldest *mambabatok* (traditional Kalinga tattooist). Many of her designs are geometric and applied using a traditional hand-tapping technique; each tattoo contains symbolic meaning specific to the Kalinga ethnic group.[30] In this case, Vitug's extension of self through the line is multiple: it is an extension of his indigenous heritage and of his body onto the canvas. The liveliness of the lines is unmistakable, too. They exist not for contour or shade but as forms of expressivity replete with their own joy and symbolic ecosystem.

The photograph on which the portrait is based was taken by an official National Women's Studies Association photographer in November 2014, during a panel discussion at the annual meeting in San Juan, Puerto Rico. Vitug came across the photograph and made the portrait several years later, while preparing a series that features his coworkers in casual situations. Though this is a portrait of me at work, I am happy. It is important, I think, that the presentation of comfort and pleasure is a through line linking this portrait and his later series. Given the elusiveness of representing Black female pleasure that I have discussed throughout this article, its presence in this portrait is significant. It allows us to rethink what constitutes pleasure, especially as it is tied to gender and race and as it brings us toward the possibilities of excess that inhere within representation itself.

In Dickinson's description of orgasm, blackness is explicitly excluded from his dual projects of revealing a norm and teaching men how to induce orgasm in women. The sensitivity toward stimulation, impressibility, implicitly tilts this aspect of the sexological project toward white women, imagining that Black sexual response is more closely related to nature, something unthought. In Masters and Johnson's focus on physiology and particular organs, the work of racialization cannot be parsed; its lines of force escape these particular contours of representation. In thinking with the places that racialization does appear, we encounter a history of extractive relationships that include the reliance on enslaved women for knowledge about anatomy and as the subjects (unable to consent) of gynecological surgery.[31] This focus on Black anatomy is further reflected in determined searches for racial difference in the clitoris and buttocks, which then become grafted onto imaginaries of behavior, as Margaret Gibson and Siobhan Somerville have argued.[32] Despite Dickinson's exclusion of Black anatomy from his *Atlas of Human Sex Anatomy*, his drawings do appear as part of the Sex Variant Study on homosexuality in New York in the 1930s, which Jennifer Terry argues attempted to map difference onto genitalia.[33]

That this exclusion and deviance are both transmitted through the line helps us reflect on how sexology itself gives us insight into the nature of portraiture and the power dynamics in which it can be mired. In Dickinson's and Masters and Johnson's failure to grapple with race, we see they are attempting to work with a concept they consider other. Portraiture born outside of this hierarchical, classificatory framework, as is the case with Vitug, might begin with the question of who is empowered to author knowledge and veer elsewhere. In the context of the sexological, Julian Carter reminds us that marginalized populations have always also attempted to author their own theories of knowledge that follow their own representational schemas:

> Anything queers (of varied races) sought to say about their own lives could be brushed off as reflecting a "savage" inability to comprehend the realities of civilized modern life, while self-representations by people of color

(of many sexualities) could be equally easily dismissed as skewed by their allegedly innate sexual coarseness and immorality. In short, racism and homophobia were mutually reinforced by their common reference to developmental failures that worked to disqualify people of color/queers from participating in the pursuit or communication of knowledge.[34]

Vitug's portrait, then, offers a corrective on multiple levels. It allows us to reread Baudrillard's description of the face as a sex organ, of which Annamarie Jagose notes, "It turns out the facial close-up is more emphatically comparable not to the genital close-up but to the genital organ per se: 'It *is* a sexual organ.'"[35] Jagose's reading allows us not only to reconsider the relation between portraiture and sexology but to also rethink what we think we know about sexuality. Vitug has not portrayed ecstasy in the conventional sense (or where a focus on orgasm might be expected to lead), but his portrait does illuminate a fleshiness that exists in excess of representational capture, what I have elsewhere called *brown jouissance*.[36] This brown jouissance oscillates between objectification, Thingification, and the production of provisional porous selfhood. In this case, intellectual labor is the cause for this excess sensuality, and I use this occasion deliberately to point to inhabitations of Black femininity that might exist outside the traditional capture of sexuality but that still traffic in erotics. This shift in perspective leads us to reimaging frameworks for thinking sexuality; we can expand what sexology's technologies of portraiture might consist of, and we can theorize the qualities of sensuality of which sexology tries to speak. In this turn toward brown jouissance we also find a theorization of race as expressive in a way that does not altogether avoid representational capture and yet does not become sedimented into something necessarily knowable. Race is part of both the negotiation of circumstance and the embodied knowledge that emerges from having lived. The shift toward expressivity as a framework allows for multiple permutations and possibilities for pleasure, sexuality, race, and representation. Each of these categories becomes unruly. The work of the portraitist, here Vitug, is ethical. Through his painted lines, he is negotiating modes of presenting these forms of expressivity while keeping them dynamic and how to make knowledge while staying attentive to the pleasures of the flesh.

Amber Jamilla Musser is professor of English at the Graduate Center, City University of New York. She is the author of *Sensational Flesh: Race, Power, and Masochism* (2014) and *Sensual Excess: Queer Femininity and Brown Jouissance* (2018).

Notes

Special thanks to Jevijoe Vitug for the portrait, Joan Lubin and Jeanne Vaccaro for their wonderful editorial comments, and the anonymous reviewers of *Social Text*.

1. I am deliberately using words that contain echoes within Black studies' focus on fugitivity, errancy, and excess.

2. In "Queer Form," Kadji Amin, Roy Pérez, and I elaborate on the importance of thinking with aesthetics in order to speak back to this racialized demand: "Artists of color are often assigned the role of testifying to the sociological conditions of their own disempowerment. They are the 'native informants' of the art world, tasked with producing art that transmits information rather than pushing aesthetic boundaries. Such a colonial tasking, however, undermines or even silences analysis of their aesthetic aims is liable to be precluded or questioned. Aesthetic innovation and formal manipulation are, however, the very substance of many of these artists' engagement with legacies of social violence. Aesthetic form offers resources of resistance to the violences of interpretation that prematurely fix the meaning of minority artistic production into prefabricated narratives" (227).

3. For more extended arguments about this, see Musser, *Sensational Flesh*; and Musser, *Sensual Excess*.

4. For a history of intimacy and marriage in the United States, see D'Emilio and Freedman, *Intimate Matters*.

5. Wright, *Sex Factor in Marriage*, 101.

6. Jagose, *Orgasmology*, 34.

7. Jagose, *Orgasmology*, 46.

8. Williams, *Hardcore*.

9. Though it was common in anatomical texts to illustrate the morphology of the clitoris and vagina, physiological illustrations of orgasm did not exist prior to Dickinson. Most sex research that occurred after Dickinson and before Masters and Johnson is more sociological in nature and presents data in numerical form. For an example, see Kinsey, *Sexual Behavior of the Human Male*.

10. Dickinson, *Atlas of Human Sex Anatomy*, vii.

11. For further investigation of the relationship between the literary and the pornographic, see Bennett and Rosario, *Solitary Pleasures*.

12. Dickinson, *Atlas of Human Sex Anatomy*, 3.

13. Dickinson, *Atlas of Human Sex Anatomy*, 92.

14. Dickinson, *Atlas of Human Sex Anatomy*, fig. 158.

15. Schuller, *Biopolitics of Feeling*, 7.

16. Schuller, *Biopolitics of Feeling*, 101.

17. Schuller, *Biopolitics of Feeling*, 109.

18. Schuller, *Biopolitics of Feeling*, 109.

19. Creadick, *Perfectly Average*, 42.

20. This precision was achieved through Masters and Johnson's employment of Ulysses, a dildo with photographic capabilities and a Plexiglas window, to literally create a window into female sexual response. In part, this shift toward film and photography was due to the belief that machines could provide unbiased "objective" data—not the subjective accounts on which Dickinson had to rely. By documenting various stages of response, Ulysses allowed Masters and Johnson to witness what happened during penetration. Extrapolating from these data, they built a case for a universal type of female sexual response. Ulysses, as a dildo, was meant to represent sex—actual sex could happen only between two people (for Masters and Johnson,

sex also happened to be heterosexual and reproductive). Though they acknowledged the potential for different responses with Ulysses versus with a partner, Masters and Johnson used data from their research to argue for its sameness: "In view of the artificial nature of the equipment, legitimate issue may be raised with the integrity of observed reaction patterns. Suffice it to say that intravaginal physiologic response corresponds in every way with previously established reaction patterns observed and recorded during hundreds of cycles in response to automanipulation" (*Human Sexual Response*, 21–22). Simultaneously arguing for the data's difference and sameness articulates the dilemma at the heart of simulation. Using the machine to simulate sex opened sex as a category and made its definition fluid. Since copulation with a machine provided the same result as human intercourse, all orgasms, no matter what the cause, were considered to be the same. This was a major contrast to Dickinson's view that intercourse could only be approximated, not replicated.

21. In outlining the parameters of their study, Masters and Johnson include "11 Negro family units" in addition to two Negro women who were evaluated without marital partners because one was a "surgical castrate" and the other had an artificial vagina (*Human Sexual Response*, 15). This is in addition to the 369 white female and 301 white male participants. In explaining this aspect of their study population, Masters and Johnson describe three of the Negro families as being of privileged backgrounds and eight as hailing from underprivileged backgrounds. The Negro sample also comes with a small disclaimer: "In view of the small number of Negro families in the study-subject population, it is obvious that the population has, over the years, been weighted toward the Caucasian rather than the Negro race" (15). The residue of race, however, is barely to be found in the rest of the study, which presents a unified portrait of female and male sexual response.

22. Desrosières, *Politics of Large Numbers*, 196.

23. Desrosières, *Politics of Large Numbers*, 214.

24. Deleuze, "Postscript on the Societies of Control."

25. Irving, *Disorders of Desire*, 90.

26. Davidson, *Emergence of Sexuality*.

27. Ricardo Montez's analysis of artist Keith Haring's use of line as a way to grapple with racial dynamics is especially helpful here. See Montez, *Keith Haring's Line*.

28. Nancy, *Pleasure in Drawing*, xii–xiii.

29. Nancy, *Pleasure in Drawing*, 10.

30. Lowe, "Reviving the Art of Filipino Tribal Tattoos."

31. For more on this history, see Ivy, "Bodies of Work"; and Snorton, *Black on Both Sides*.

32. Gibson, "Clitoral Corruption"; Somerville, *Queering the Color Line*.

33. Terry, *American Obsession*.

34. Carter, "On Mother-Love," 124.

35. Jagose, *Orgasmology*, 145.

36. Musser, *Sensual Excess*.

References

Amin, Kadji, Amber Jamilla Musser, and Roy Pérez. "Queer Form: Aesthetics, Race, and the Violences of the Social." *ASAP/Journal* 2, no. 2 (2017): 227–39.

Bennett, Paula, and Vernon Rosario, eds. *Solitary Pleasures: The Historical, Literary, and Artistic Discourses of Autoeroticism*. New York: Psychology Press, 1995.

Carter, Julian. "On Mother-Love: History, Queer Theory, and Nonlesbian Identity." *Journal of the History of Sexuality* 14, no. 1 (2005): 107–38.

Creadick, Anna G. *Perfectly Average: The Pursuit of Normality in Postwar America.* Amherst: University of Massachusetts Press, 2010.

Davidson, Arnold. *The Emergence of Sexuality.* Cambridge, MA: Harvard University Press, 2001.

Deleuze, Gilles. "Postscript on the Societies of Control." *October,* no. 59 (1992): 3–7.

D'Emilio, John, and Estelle Freedman. *Intimate Matters: A History of Sexuality in America.* New York: Harper and Row, 1988.

Desrosières, Alain. *The Politics of Large Numbers: A History of Statistical Reasoning.* Cambridge, MA: Harvard University Press, 2002.

Dickinson, Robert Latou. *Atlas of Human Sex Anatomy.* Baltimore: Williams and Wilkins, 1949.

Gibson, Margaret. "Clitoral Corruption: Body Metaphors and American Doctors' Constructions of Female Homosexuality, 1870–1900." In *Science and Homosexualities,* edited by Vernon Rosario, 108–32. New York: Routledge, 1997.

Irving, Janice. *Disorders of Desire: Sexuality and Gender in Modern American Sexology.* Philadelphia: Temple University Press, 2005.

Ivy, Nicole. "Bodies of Work: A Meditation on Medical Imaginaries and Enslaved Women." *Souls* 18, no. 1 (2016): 11–31.

Jagose, Annamarie. *Orgasmology.* Durham, NC: Duke University Press, 2012.

Kinsey, Alfred. *Sexual Behavior of the Human Male.* Bloomington: Indiana University Press, 1948.

Lowe, Aya. "Reviving the Art of Filipino Tribal Tattoos." BBC News, May 27, 2014. www.bbc.com/news/world-asia-27539510.

Masters, William, and Virginia Johnson. *Human Sexual Response.* Boston: Little Brown, 1966.

Montez, Ricardo. *Keith Haring's Line: Race and the Performance of Desire.* Durham, NC: Duke University Press, 2020.

Musser, Amber Jamilla. *Sensational Flesh: Race, Power, and Masochism.* New York: New York University Press, 2014.

Musser, Amber Jamilla. *Sensual Excess: Queer Femininity and Brown Jouissance.* New York: New York University Press, 2018.

Nancy, Jean Luc. *The Pleasure in Drawing.* Translated Phillip Armstrong. New York: Fordham University Press, 2012.

Schuller, Kyla. *The Biopolitics of Feeling: Race, Sex, and Science in the Nineteenth Century.* Durham, NC: Duke University Press, 2018.

Snorton, C. Riley. *Black on Both Sides: A Racial History of Trans Identity.* Minneapolis: University of Minnesota Press, 2017.

Somerville, Siobhan. *Queering the Color Line: Race and the Invention of Homosexuality.* Durham, NC: Duke University Press, 2000.

Terry, Jennifer. *An American Obsession: Science, Medicine, and Homosexuality in Modern Society.* Chicago: University of Chicago Press, 1999.

Williams, Linda. *Hardcore: Power, Pleasure, and "The Frenzy of the Visible."* Berkeley: University of California Press, 1989.

Wright, Helena. *The Sex Factor in Marriage: A Book for Those Who Are or Are about to Be Married.* New York: Vanguard, 1931.

On Stalling and Turning

A Wayward Genealogy for a
Binary-Abolitionist Public Toilet Project

Susan Stryker

1.

I have watched brown pelicans gliding serenely over the Pacific Ocean for
hours on end. They offer a study in economy of motion: wings fixed, they
surf the thermal currents circulating between sea and sky, skimming and
soaring to scan subsurface waters for the schooling fish on which they
feed. Suddenly, on high with prey in sight below, a bird will tilt its wings to
stall and hang midair for an astonishing instant of utter stillness. It tucks
into a turn to fall like a dropped spear and vanish beneath the waves, only
to reappear moments later with the pouch beneath its bill filled with the
squirming life it swallows. However often I see this act repeated, it never
fails to thrill me.

2.

The following vignettes offer a series of stalls and turns in reference to
spatial imaginaries.

3.

I grew up in an active-duty military family. For three years, 1968–71,
when I was between the ages of seven and ten, we were stationed at East-
man Barracks, a small US Army base that occupied much of the former
grounds of the first Nazi concentration camp, in Dachau, which served as
a template for all the camps that followed. One section of the old camp had
become a memorial, and another served as housing for Turkish *gastarbe-*

Social Text 148 · Vol. 39, No. 3 · September 2021
DOI 10.1215/01642472-9034432 © 2021 Duke University Press

iter, but the US Army simply kept much of it for its own use in the postwar occupation of Europe. The base commander lived in the old commandant's house, and officers lived in spacious two-story duplexes that members of the Waffen-SS had once called home while they trained their peers from throughout the Third Reich in the practical art of operating concentration camps. We lived with other enlisted men's families in postwar apartment buildings, while single enlisted men lived in a barracks whose exterior still bore a bas relief of the Reichsadler, an eagle perched atop a wreath encircling a swastika. I came to know the base's physical layout well through my first job, delivering the *Stars and Stripes* newspaper early every morning. Sometimes I sacked groceries for tips at the commissary. Sometimes I even got to stock the shelves, and I loved using the sticker gun to put prices on the cartons and cans. On such days, I was allowed to enter the cavernous warehouse area behind the retail space, where I could see the pallets of foodstuffs and household goods that had been unloaded at the dock. On other days, I could hop the fence that separated the army base from the memorial to visit the museum there and look at an old photograph of the same building the commissary now occupied. It showed piles of corpses unloaded onto pallets on the same dock where I stickered boxes of breakfast cereal.

Living as a child on the former camp's grounds introduced me to more than the blunt reality of the Holocaust's reduction of living persons to ash and bone, though it did not supply me with names and concepts for what I encountered there. I learned by dwelling in and moving through a built space that had been organized in a particular way that beliefs and worldviews manifest in a spatial dimension but that the architectonics of a given space are more fundamental than whatever program activates it. I saw that a certain fungibility could pertain even between seemingly binarized opposites—Allies/Nazis, us/them, persons/things. I would go so far as to say, retroactively, that I recognized a relation between spatial schema and the imaginaries through which subjects and populations cohere—a floor plan, if you will, that obviates programmatic distinctions between liberal and fascist societies and orchestrates the necropolitical project that underlies sexology along with its eugenic and race-science kin.

I ask myself, Was this early capacity to recognize the capacity of any given organization of space to accommodate a variety of programs a consequence of my already self-aware sense of being trans?

4.

I've dabbled with a creative practice since the early 1990s: short fiction, spoken word, performance art, autotheory, digital media. My first slapdash and poorly documented wall work, part of Jordy Jones's 1995 *Art.*

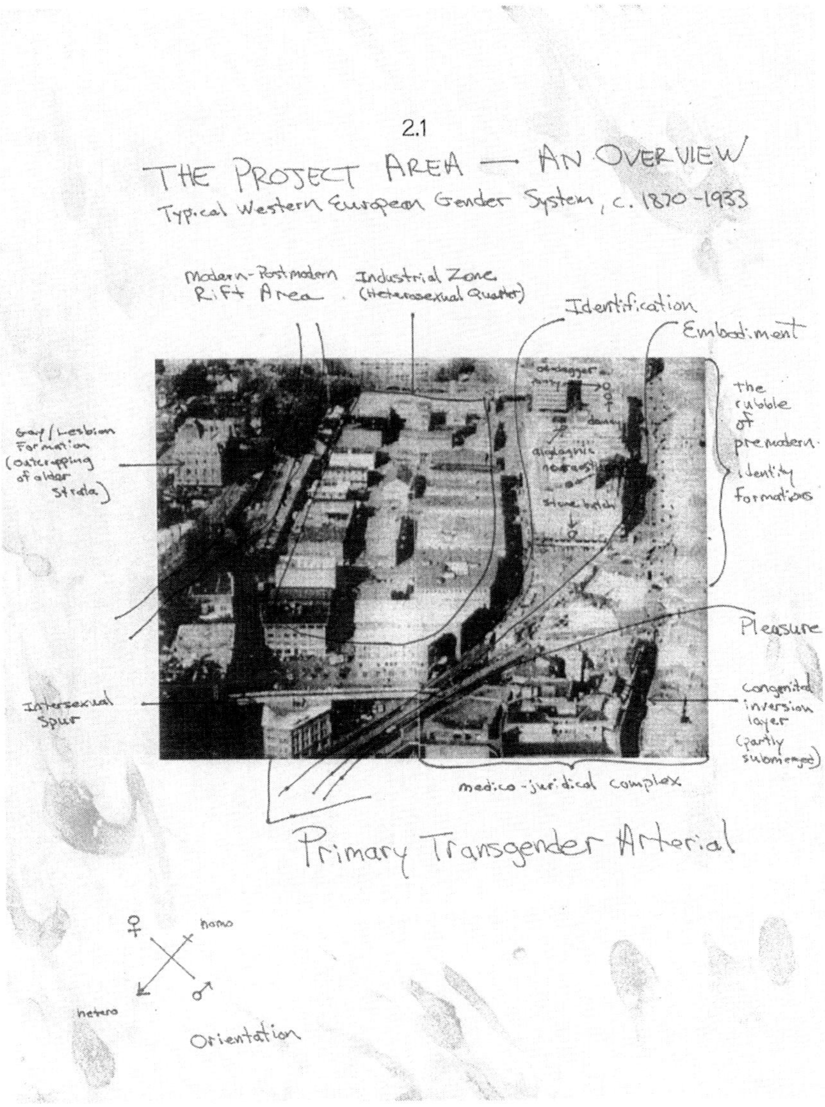
2.1
THE PROJECT AREA — AN OVERVIEW
Typical Western European Gender System, c. 1870-1933
Modern-Postmodern Rift Area
Industrial Zone (Heterosexual Quarter)
Identification
Embodiment
The rubble of premodern identity formations
Gay/Lesbian Formation (outcropping of older strata)
Pleasure
Intersexual Spur
congenital inversion layer (partly submerged)
medico-juridical complex
Primary Transgender Arterial
homo
hetero
Orientation

Figure 1. Susan Stryker, *Transsexual Bridge City* (1995). Digitally altered and photocopied images and ink on foam board, 8.5 × 11 in.

Crime group show at BUILD Gallery in San Francisco, was *Transsexual Bridge City* (figs. 1–3). My "crime" was the appropriation of architect Bernard Tschumi's proposal for the revitalization of the old industrial core of Lausanne, Switzerland, as published in his book *Event-Cities*. I was inspired not only by Tschumi's insight into how the organization of space generates some events and forecloses others but also by his sense of how to repurpose the circulation space of the bridges that characterize the

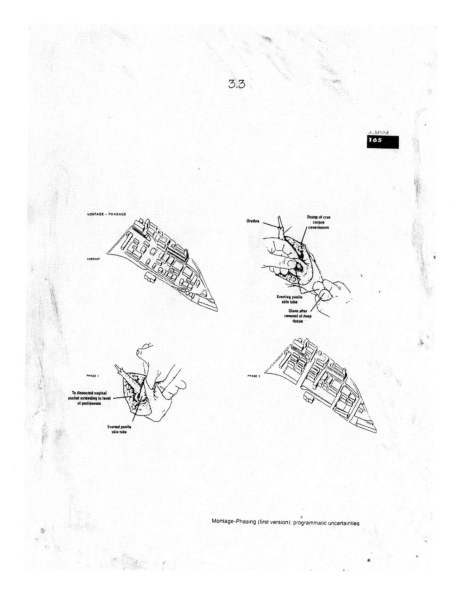

Figure 2. Susan Stryker, *Transsexual Bridge City* (1995). Digitally altered and photocopied images and ink on foam board, 8.5 × 11 in.

built environment of the city's uneven topography as spaces of occupation: a "cross-programming" of the functions of moving and dwelling that resonated for me with the phenomenology of transsexual embodiment. I overlaid an aerial view of the city with the schema of sexuality—the manufacturing zone of heterosexual reproduction delimited by the "primary transgender arterial" that sliced through the built environment and exceeded its frame—and suggested, through the appropriation of archi-

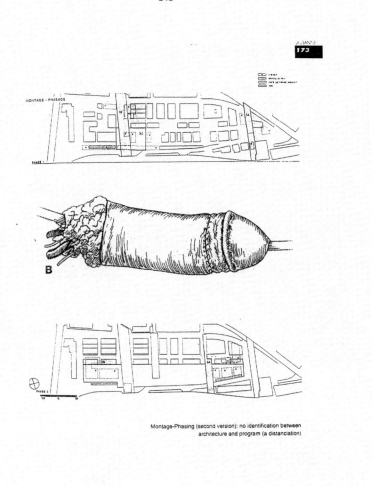

Figure 3. Susan Stryker, *Transsexual Bridge City* (1995). Digitally altered and photocopied images and ink on foam board, 8.5 × 11 in.

tectural concepts, transversal connections across scales between city planning and genital surgery.

Later I discover Bernard Cache's *Earth Moves: The Furnishing of Territories*, a work of Deleuzian architectural theory that likewise used the topography and built environment of Lausanne to develop a conceptual vocabulary of concrete abstractions for analyzing movement and space: the inflection point between structure and ground, the frame of the structure as a selector of movement-images, and the vector of movable objects passing through the space. Through it, I grasped underlying similarities among architecture, embodiment, and cinema that enabled my own methodological turn toward filmmaking as another way of knowing.

Spatial theory drawn from creative work played a direct role in my research into the subject of my first film, *Screaming Queens* (1995), codirected with Victor Silverman, about the Compton's Cafeteria Riot of 1966, in which trans women, street queens, gay hustlers, and unsheltered street youth fought back against police oppression in San Francisco's Tenderloin district, at the corner of Turk and Taylor Streets. There was scant textual evidence of the event—no newspaper stories or television coverage, no primary documents such as police records—other than one substantive retrospective account published in 1972 and a few scattered and oblique hints in the gay and lesbian community press. In the absence of such evidence, I turned away from my training as a historian and turned toward an analysis of the built environment at the level of the city and the neighborhood to understand how, as suggested by Tschumi, a city space might generate an event. I came to understand how the Tenderloin became the city's sex-work ghetto, how trans women facing employment and housing discrimination wound up living there and doing sex work, and how Compton's Cafeteria functioned as a neighborhood gathering spot for the trans women living in the SRO hotels clustered in a half-block radius around it. In doing so, I came to understand the structure of the urban environment as enabling of particular kinds of events, a theoretical insight that lent plausibility to the sole uncorroborated print-based account of the riot, and that allowed subsequent verification of it through community-based oral history research.

5.

How might the recent resurgence of transphobic feminism, which takes special aim at the phantasmatic figure of the trans woman as male sex predator stalking the sex-segregated "lady's room" or public toilet, be approached as a spatial problem that informs practices of stalling and turning?

Patricia Elliot and Lawrence Lyons offer an astute psychoanalytic reading of feminist transphobia as symptomatic of a particular structuring of feminine subjectivity.[1] Symptoms speak truths that are not consciously or intentionally expressed; they are unconscious forms of knowledge that don't know themselves as such and hence are prone to perpetually repeat themselves. Like dreams and other formations of unconscious processes, symptoms "appear with a vividness that goes beyond typical representations of lived experience" and express what Jacques Lacan called a "passion for ignorance" that protects the subject from a trauma that threatens to unmake it.[2] The trans woman in the phobic feminist fantasy functions as a mask that covers a foundational wounding to which the fearful subject remains attached, from which she seeks to detach and heal, and who in failing to accomplish her own self-repair repeats the symptom of self-defensive transphobic attack. Following Slavoj Žižek's analysis of anti-Semitism as a symptom of an unattainable fantasy of social purity that produces "the Jew" as its uncanny other, Elliot and Lyons read feminist transphobia as the symptom of a similarly unattainable fantasy that generates a caricature of the transwoman as its Golem-like double. They argue that the unmooring of symbolic categories of sex by those who cross its boundaries represents what must be repressed if certain forms of wounded attachment to feminist womanhood are to be maintained.

The Lacanian theorist and clinician Oren Gozlan has written insightfully regarding how public discourse on transgender and transsexual issues plays out disproportionately in relation to the space of the gender-segregated public toilet, only to become "stalled on the stall" through the interference of transphobic fantasy.[3] This stalled discourse, he contends, "reflects the fact that transsexuality continues to haunt us as a dilemma concerning the universal conundrum of sexual difference and gender identity as constituted through complex negotiations of psychic and sociosymbolic demands essential to our constitution as desiring, embodied subjects." To the extent that "the presence of the transsexual in the bathroom reminds us that our bodies are not given, transparent," or intrinsically legible, Gozlan continues, the public toilet becomes a productive space for playing out "phantasies of control and expulsion, abjection, anxiety, relief, anticipation, and hate," as well as for understanding how "these unconscious resonances stall our capacity to think."

Both Gozlan and Elliot and Lyon frame their understanding of transphobia in the sphere of the public toilet within the architectonic schema of sexual difference—that is, of taking a psychical position in relation to the question of difference posed by the Lacanian phallus—which the "urinary segregation" of the binary-gendered public toilet itself replicates and reproduces in the built environment. Transphobia, in this view, is the fear of confronting the other that has crossed out of its proper place and thereby threatens to undo difference itself and thus unmake the subject. This fear is cathected onto the penis as phallus in a reactive fantasy that imagines penises in places that contradict the logic of sexual difference—on the otherwise feminine appearance of the trans woman, and in the presence of such bodies in the sex-segregated space of the women's public toilet—which then informs the fear of rape as the ultimate manifestation of a penis out of place. This is despite the lack of empirical instances of trans women or cross-dressed men preying on cisgender women and girls in sex-segregated public toilets.[4]

6.

The remainder of this article suggests how the transsexual promise of undoing difference might be actualized differently, in a nonphobic register, in ways that potentially decouple it from the schema of biopower that instrumentalizes difference to create the hierarchies that maldistribute access to the means of life according to morphological imaginaries of sex and race. It turns in a different direction, and does so precisely by delinking the architectural floor plan of the public toilet from the architectonics of a psychical sex binary. This is the sociopolitical project spatialized in the Stalled! binary-abolitionist public toilet redesign project.[5]

Stalled! had its origin in 2015, when Joel Sanders, an architect in private practice in New York, as well as a professor of practice at the Yale School of Architecture, reached out to rekindle our lapsed collegial relationship. Years earlier, while working on *Screaming Queens* and deep into my research on the urban geography of sexuality in San Francisco, we had met through our mutual involvement with the Arcus Endowment for the Study of Sexuality and the Built Environment at the UC Berkeley College of Environmental Design. Joel had previously edited the anthology 1996 *STUD: Architectures of Masculinity*, and his architectural practice included designing nonheteronormative domestic spaces; he was as interested in queer, trans, and feminist theory as I was eager for a deeper engagement with architecture and spatial theory. We were each looking for ways to harness our personal and professional interests to social justice activisms we both cared about, and we decided to collaborate on some project of mutual interest. Contentious and seemingly intractable public debates about "transgender toilets" were then flaring up in Texas, North Carolina, and elsewhere, and we noted how mainstream media coverage and public discourse did not address this issue from an architectural perspective. They focused on who should be allowed in which restroom, rather than on how the floor plan itself could be altered. We coauthored a short academic article for *South Atlantic Quarterly* and collaborated on an op-ed piece for the *Los Angeles Times*, both of which proposed some preliminary solutions to the problems caused by sex-segregated public toilets, and we began actively researching even better designs.[6] As a more ambitious project began to take shape through our collaboration, we brought onboard Terry Kogan, professor of law at University of Utah, for his legal expertise regarding antitransgender discrimination regarding public toilet access.

The concept of the gender-neutral public toilet is of course not original to the Stalled! project.[7] The project's distinctiveness lies in its theoretical motivations and research-driven design practice, in its conviction that innovative architecture can solve social problems, and in the actual spatial solutions being proposed. Moreover, Stalled! was envisioned from the outset as an opportunity for sociopolitical intervention through the development not just of a practical public toilet redesign but of educational materials, professional best-practices guidelines, a replicable methodology for inclusive design research, and an activist campaign to remove barriers to gender-neutral public toilets from the International Plumbing Code.

In our public presentations at colleges and universities, we disseminated our research findings on the history of gender-segregated public toilets in the West, particularly in the United States.[8] We quickly learned that such facilities are of surprisingly recent origin. Before the advent of indoor plumbing, there were chamber pots for use indoors, and privies or outhouses outdoors, neither of which were gender segregated. Privies for family homes were often communal, with different-sized holes to accommodate larger or smaller bodies of adults and children. The first commercial building in the United States with indoor plumbing, the Tremont House hotel in Boston, built in 1829, had gender-segregated dining rooms and parlors for single ladies and gentlemen, but its public toilets were non-gender-specific rows of private single-user stalls with a common washing-up area.[9] Gender-segregated public toilets were virtually unknown in the United States before the 1880s. Their proliferation at that time was due in part to rising numbers of women in the paid workforce and the need to accommodate the act of eliminating bodily waste without female workers having to leave the workplace. But the perceived desirability of sex/gender segregation was itself a reflection of nineteenth-century ideas among white elites about social progress, evolutionary theory, and the "sciences" of sex and race.[10]

Well into the eighteenth century, a "one-sex" model of the human body found numerous adherents in western European societies, with different genital shapes imagined as expressing greater or lesser degrees of perfection of a single paradigmatic body plan, that is, the idea that the female was a less perfect version of the default-male human form. That paradigm had shifted markedly by the nineteenth century, when it became more common to think of men and women as practically two distinct kinds of biological creatures. This newly dominant binary model of biological sex merged with evolutionary theories to produce a socially powerful idea: that heightened sexual differentiation was a sign of evolutionary advancement. This discourse narrated a progression from "primitive" organisms that were either asexual or hermaphroditic, through many "lower" animals whose sex was not immediately apparent to untrained human observers, to "higher" forms of life, such as *Homo sapiens*, that tended toward ever clearer and more highly specialized forms of sex difference. The appearance of the "ladies' room" in this context, in other words, was not just a way to speed the accumulation of capital through the more efficient exploitation of female industrial labor, or simply a prudish Victorian strategy for protecting the refined sensibilities of the frailer and gentler sex; it was also thought to represent the progress of civilization and the perfection of the human race.[11] The same beliefs about greater biological sex differentiation being a sign of evolutionary progress that underpinned the emergence of the ladies' room informed the racist logic underpinning the racial segregation of public toilets: doors marked "Men," "Women," and "Colored" displayed the obvious but unstated belief that sex differentiation was a privilege of whiteness.

The development of sex-segregated public toilets materialized psychically fraught concepts of sexuated subjectivity, as well as deeply held and largely unacknowledged beliefs about the nature of the biological body and the relation of particular kinds of bodies to the collective body politic.[12] As previously marginalized social groups have fought for the ability to take up space in the public sphere, it is thus no surprise that those who feel threatened by or opposed to those groups have expressed their hostility to change by focusing their fears and resentments on the public toilet. In the 1950s and 1960s, the abolition of "colored" restrooms was a prominent goal of the Black civil rights movement. In the 1970s, resistance to women's liberation and opposition to passage of the Equal Rights Amendment generated a moral panic about "unisex toilets." In the 1980s, during the early days of the AIDS epidemic, a similar panic emerged around the fear of infected gay men contaminating innocent heterosexual men by using the same public lavatories. Disability rights activists succeeded in passing the Americans with Disabilities Act in 1990, only to encounter ongoing resistance to actually making public toilets more accessible to people who are not normatively able-bodied. In each instance, the public restroom, by virtue of it being a physical space, transformed an immaterial concern over embodied difference into a tangible peril and became the setting for nightmarish fantasies of so-called normal citizens being compelled to physically interact with others whose mere presence in that space was considered a danger.

In recent years, public restrooms have become the site of another moral panic sparked by the specter of accommodating transgender and nonbinary individuals. Transgender issues have exploded into greater visibility since the 1990s, and they approached a watershed in legal recognition and social acceptance in the United States during the final years of Barack Obama's presidency. A backlash to these developments began building around 2013, including numerous regressive measures related to public toilet access, notably the "No on 1" campaign to repeal HERO, the Houston Equal Rights Ordinance, in 2015 and North Carolina's notorious House Bill 2 in 2016. In 2017 the Trump administration rescinded Title IX protections for transgender students put forth by the Obama administration that mandated allowing them to use the toilet at their public schools that best matched their gender identity and expression, and the Supreme Court declined to hear the public-school toilet access case on behalf of Virginia high school student Gavin Grimm, which once had promised to settle the question of formal legal equality for transgender citizens. With a fresh wave of "religious liberty" bills, laws seeking to criminalize supportive medical services for transgender youth and bar them from athletic competitions, and regressive policies on bureaucratic name and gender change sweeping the country as of 2020, the future does not look bright for the recognition and accommodation of transgender people as an identifiable minority. All the more reason, then, to advance another strategy for addressing social justice concerns.[13]

7.

The so-called debates about transgender access to sex-segregated public are intractable precisely because, as suggested above, they are not rational—rather, they are enmeshed with psychical defenses against confronting sexual difference, which become powerful ideological props for sustaining the racist and sexist inequalities necessary for the accumulation of capital through the exploitation of racially and sexually hierarchized bodies. The Stalled! project attempts to intervene in this situation not by crafting a better argument for equality and access, or by offering psychotherapy to people whose ability to encounter the actually existing diversity of the world is limited by fear of an unreal threat, but by materially reorganizing the space of the restroom. It reconfigures the relationship between public and private in ways that can feel less threatening and more engaging while also abolishing barriers based on binaries that can result in harm not just to transgender bodies but to cisgender women and girls, as well as many kinds of people whose bodies are "noncompliant," either willfully or unavoidably, with discriminatory social norms.

The first step of our design process was to examine the most common approach to implementing all-gender restrooms—the single-user solution. It supplements existing sex-segregated restrooms with a third, single-occupancy bathroom labeled gender neutral. Although a step in the right direction, the single-user solution has two drawbacks: it naturalizes the gender binary by separating "men" and "women" in two rooms, which reinforces the essentialist notion of gender identity and expression as an effect of biology, and it segregates all difference from the dominant binary form into the supplemental third space. In doing so, it subjects those with bodies that do not conform to dominant notions of embodiment—not only trans and gender-nonconforming people but also people with disabilities—to a "separate but equal" logic that is never equal and that contributes to social isolation and stigma. Although a well-intentioned alternative to

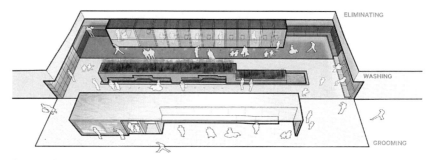

ELIMINATING

WASHING

GROOMING

Figure 4. Stalled! gender-neural public toilet project. Design concept for high-traffic areas such as airports. Courtesy of the Stalled! project.

sex-segregated multiuser public toilets, the single-user restroom is not sufficient to the need.

Stalled! therefore advocates an alternative multiuser solution that treats the restroom as a single open space, replacing the typical stalls whose revealing gaps compromise privacy with floor-to-ceiling partitions and communal areas for washing and grooming. This solution has the advantage of consolidating a greater number of people in one rather than two rooms, so that users can create a more populated and diverse "commons" that reduces the risk of violence, while ensuring that gender-nonconforming people are not stuck between two options that do not align with their identities. It better meets the needs of trans and nonbinary people while also increasing access for a wide range of nonnormative bodies traditionally neglected in public restrooms: caregivers of different genders than those they care for, the elderly, people who are nursing, parents with small children of a different gender, religious minorities in need of spaces for ritual cleansing, people needing privacy to self-administer medication or attend to health needs, and people with disabilities or nontypical bodies. Rather than focus on gender alone, Stalled! uses transgender issues and the concept of "binary abolitionism" as points of departure for a much broader reimagining of the public sphere.

Stalled! has developed a public toilet design that takes existing multiuser approaches a step further by addressing not just the sex/gender binary but the relationship of public/private, by changing the placement of walls and partitions (fig. 4). Drawing inspiration from pre-nineteenth-century historical precedents, we reconceived restrooms as animated communal spaces that promote social interaction among a spectrum of differently embodied people. Our prototype for high-traffic areas such as airports eliminates all walls and partitions except one: the toilet stall. We began by removing the existing plumbing stack wall and treated the bathroom as one nongendered open space. Then we eliminated the cor-

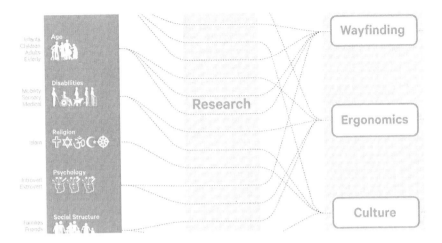

Figure 5. Stalled! gender-neutral public toilet project, research methodology. Courtesy of the Stalled! project.

ridor wall to make the bathroom a porous extension of the corridor. Farthest from the corridor, we added blocks of fully enclosed stalls of three sizes—standard, ambulatory, and ADA compliant—as well as caregiving rooms equipped with toilet, sink, and changing tables that allow for caregiving between people of different genders. Those who want privacy can retreat into alcoves for breastfeeding, administering medical procedures such insulin injections, meditation, and prayer. We next added communal grooming and washing areas off the main circulation path. The public restroom thereby becomes an open, agora-like precinct adjacent to the main concourse that is animated by three parallel activity zones, dedicated respectively to grooming, washing, and eliminating.

Within this basic spatial layout, we needed to address further design elements. Our challenge was to find a shared lexicon of materials, lighting, and technologies that would allow various user groups to mingle freely in public space while promoting safety and hygiene. In response, we developed a rubric for implementing a more widely applicable inclusive design research methodology (fig. 5). Three factors guided our design decisions:

1. Wayfinding: devising systems that use color, texture, and lighting in lieu of signage alone to help people with physical and sensory disabilities navigate public space.
2. Ergonomics: integrating shared elements like counters at different heights that encourage social mixing.
3. Culture: making design decisions that enhance physical and psychological well-being to counteract culturally learned feelings of embarrassment and shame that bathrooms can evoke in users.

The outcome of this design process was to propose slip-resistant sheets of diamond plate, tile, and rubber to differentiate the three activity zones for eliminating, washing, and grooming, and to paint each a different shade of the same color as a guide for the visually impaired. After debating the merits of different color options, we chose blue based on research that indicates that it is soothing; is associated with water, health, and hygiene; and supplies a complementary background color for deaf signing because it contrasts with skin tones. Locating the toilet stalls into consolidated rows at the back of the facility offers the greatest possible acoustic and visual privacy for acts of eliminating bodily waste. Each stall has a recessed floor light that turns on when entered and turns off when exited to allow users to see if stalls are occupied. From inside each stall, users can observe their surroundings by looking through a band of blue one-way mirrors located at seated eye level. Stalls contain low-flush composting toilets that treat human waste through aerobic decomposition, with self-raising seats that mitigate accidental or inconsiderate urination on seating surfaces by users who stand to urinate. Inset floor lights indicate the location of motion-activated faucets in the washing area, where water flows into inclined splash planes placed at different ergonomic heights, which is then collected and cleaned in a bioremediating planter before being recycled. The scent of plants and the ambient sounds of flowing water help mask bodily odors and sounds. The overall effect is that as users circulate from one activity zone to the next, passing from the outermost grooming station to the innermost toilet wall and back again, they experience a multisensory gradient that takes them from public to private, open to closed, smooth to coarse, dry to wet, acoustically reverberant to sound absorptive, ambient to spot lighting. By taking transgender embodiment as a point of departure and binary abolitionism as a principle, our spatial design process culminated in new formal and material possibilities for reimagining and reconfiguring public space in a way that increases the common good.

8.

March 17, 2020. As of today, I have completed the first draft of this article. I had left the United States exactly two weeks earlier, on March 3, for a long-planned nine-day trip to Helsinki, Finland; St. Petersburg, Russia; and Tallinn, Estonia, during my spring break at Yale University, where I am a visiting professor team-teaching an architecture seminar titled "Non-compliant Bodies" with my colleague Joel Sanders. At the time of my departure from the United States, the COVID-19 pandemic seemed like something about which to remain alert but that was still half a world

Figure 6. Public toilet, Helsinki Public Library, 2020. Photograph by Susan Stryker.

away. During my trip, I spoke to packed lecture halls, returned the hugs and handshakes of well-wishers, enjoyed socializing with friends and colleagues, ate out, took public transit, and explored places I hadn't visited before. It was cosmopolitan life as usual. In Helsinki, I was delighted to patronize the gender-neutral public restroom in the public library, which implements many of the design recommendations that emerged from the Stalled! project (fig. 6). Today, only two weeks later, the sense of "public" itself has radically changed. Social distancing, not social mixing, is most in need of a design solution. The mayor of New York City, where I've lived this past year, announced earlier this morning that the city should brace for economic conditions on par with those of the Great Depression, while the *New York Times* is calling for an emergency popular mobilization on par with the efforts of World War II. The city I call my home, San Francisco, issued a "shelter in place" directive yesterday. And yet, even today, my Twitter feed is being trolled by TERFs (trans-exclusionary radical feminists) and "gender-critical" feminists who think it's dreadfully important to tell me that I am a man.

On March 16, 2020, London's Imperial College COVID-19 Response Team, in coordination with the World Health Organization and other expert research units, issued a report suggesting that, if left to run its course unchecked, the pandemic could claim approximately 2.2 million lives in the United States, while with more drastic forms of suppression—the likes and lengths of which would be historically unprecedented—there would still likely be tens or hundreds of thousands of untimely deaths. The report concluded with this somber statement: "However, we emphasise that is not at all certain that suppression will succeed long term; no public health intervention with such disruptive effects on society has been previously attempted for such a long duration of time. How populations and societies will respond remains unclear."[14] I had to read it twice to catch the typo—the omission of "it" in the first line between "that" and "is." After having spent so much time in recent days thinking in a psychoanalytic mode, I couldn't help but see the uncorrected slip as parapraxis, a telling misperformance with an unconscious root: *it*, pronominal stand-in for nothing in particular and everything in general as subject of the verb whose infinitive form is *to be*. Did the text stall at the word that would refer to this moment of existence, finding it unutterable? Did *it* remain unwritten because thought had nowhere left to turn?

9.

My thoughts return to the pelicans hanging over the Pacific Ocean, poised midair in preparation for their hungry corkscrew dive, their plunge figuring for me my sense of gender transness: of stalling in relation to the question of sexual difference, of turning not in fear of my own dissolution but, rather, in anticipation of moving along a different axis to traverse new phases of mattering, transitioning from a social atmosphere in surrender to an aqueous abyss that can hold no stable line and thus become a space of transformation—a necessary yet unbreathable space, hostile to one's survival, where one might nevertheless retrieve a life that sustains a life even as death passes through it.

Transness as a concept makes sense only in relation to a spatial configuration on which the logic of the term depends: it requires difference and separation as a precondition of its transversal operations, even as it demonstrates how other arrangements—other floor plans, not just of sex and gender but of space and time and sociality—are possible. To figure new bodies and patterns of movement, to craft space in ways that transform relations with others, is a technical problem of design and engineering; to unleash desire for a collective life that might carry us across the fear of our own undoing is by far the harder challenge, but it is the challenge of our times.

Susan Stryker is Barbara Lee Distinguished Chair in Women's Leadership at Mills College and professor emerita of women's and gender studies at the University of Arizona. She is executive editor of *TSQ: Transgender Studies Quarterly* and author of *Transgender History: The Roots of Today's Revolution* (2017).

Notes

1. Elliot and Lyons, "Transphobia as Symptom."
2. All quotes in this paragraph are from Elliot and Lyons, "Transphobia as Symptom," 359–60.
3. All quotes in this paragraph are from Gozlan, "Stalled on the Stall," 452–53.
4. Steinmetz, "Bathroom 'Predators.'"
5. Stalled!, "Historical Context."
6. Stryker, "Everyone Poops"; Sanders and Stryker, "Stalled."
7. Much of the text that follows on the Stalled! project is adapted from the project website, www.stalled.online, collaboratively written and produced by Joel Sanders, Susan Stryker, Terry Kogan, and Seb Choe.
8. Sanders, Choe, and Stryker, "The Stalled! Project."
9. Yuko, "Glamorous, Sexist History of the Women's Restroom Lounge."
10. Kogan, *Sex-Separation in Public Restrooms.*
11. Schuller, *Biopolitics of Feeling.*
12. See Cavanagh, *Queering Bathrooms.*
13. Sanders, Choe, and Stryker, "The Stalled! Project."
14. Ferguson et al., "Impact of Non-pharmaceutical Interventions," 16.

References

Cavanagh, Sheila L. *Queering Bathrooms.* Toronto: University of Toronto Press, 2010.
Elliot, Patricia, and Lawrence Lyons. "Transphobia as Symptom: Fear of the 'Unwoman.'" *TSQ* 4, nos. 3–4 (2017): 358–83.
Ferguson, Neil M., et al. "Impact of Non-pharmaceutical Interventions (NPIs) to Reduce COVID-19 Mortality and Healthcare Demand." Imperial College Covid-19 Response Team, March 16, 2020. www.imperial.ac.uk/media/imperial -college/medicine/sph/ide/gida-fellowships/Imperial-College-COVID19-NPI -modelling-16-03-2020.pdf.
Gozlan, Oren. "Stalled on the Stall: Reflections on a Strained Discourse." *TSQ* 4, nos. 3–4 (2017): 451–71.
Kogan, Terry S. "Sex-Separation in Public Restrooms: Law, Architecture, and Gender." *Michigan Journal of Gender and Law* 14, no. 1. repository.law.umich.edu /mjgl/vol14/iss1/1.
Sanders, Joel, and Susan Stryker. "Stalled: Gender Neutral Public Toilets." *South Atlantic Quarterly* 115, no. 4 (2016): 779–88.
Sanders, Joel, Seb Choe, and Susan Stryker. "The Stalled! Project, A Conversation between Joel Sanders, Seb Choe and Susan Stryker." Mills College Trans Studies Speaker Series, Wednesday, October 21, 2020. performingarts.mills.edu /broadcasts/2020/sanders-choe.php.
Schuller, Kyla. *The Biopolitics of Feeling.* Durham, NC: Duke University Press, 2017.
Stalled! "Historical Context." April 2, 2021. www.stalled.online/historicalcontext.
Steinmetz, Katy. "Why LGBT Advocates Say Bathroom 'Predators' Argument Is

a Red Herring." *Time*, May 2, 2016, time.com/4314896/transgender-bathroom
-bill-male-predators-argument/.

Stryker, Susan. "Everyone Poops. No One Should Be Stigmatized or Criminalized
When They Answer Nature's Call." *Los Angeles Times*, April 30, 2016.

Tschumi, Bernard. *Event-Cities*. Cambridge, MA: MIT Press, 1994.

Yuko, Elizabeth. "The Glamorous, Sexist History of the Women's Restroom
Lounge." Bloomberg Citylab, December 3, 2018. www.bloomberg.com/news
/features/2018-12-03/the-rise-and-fall-of-the-women-s-restroom-lounge.

Four Gestures toward a Trans-Mad Aesthetic of Space

Lucas Crawford

> Uh, I had to take a break from work 'cause, uh, I went mental. And, uh . . .
> My friend told me, hey, you're talking a little too fast, having a lot of shit
> ideas. Uh, why don't you get in my Ford Flex, and I'll, uh, motor you over
> to the public storage. And, uh . . . I went into a psychiatric facility, which,
> if you haven't been, uh, don't feel bad if you go, and, uh . . . They're
> uniformly awful. You're not at the wrong one. They're all bad, they're
> all bad. Uh . . . It's as if an art director came in and said, "Okay, I want
> to break five more chairs, and then we need . . . Uh, at least three pieces
> taken out of every puzzle. And . . . The big screen TV, let's have it playing
> *Ultimate Fighting Championships* at maximum volume, lose the remote."
> —Maria Bamford, *Old Baby*

To best access the remainder of this essay, the author invites readers to
suspend the belief, should they hold it, that psychiatric inpatient treatment is necessarily a human or humane regimen at its core. Please enter!
Don't worry about your shoes. Unlike a psych ward, you are free to leave
whenever you so choose.

I make this invitation via two quotidian but illustrative anecdotes—
one my own, the other belonging to comedian Maria Bamford—with the
purpose of beginning to reframe psychiatric confinement as, in part, a
matter of spatial control. First, in her 2017 Netflix comedy special, Bamford refers to psychiatric institutions as "public storage." Further, she
recalls telling her friends that she may sometimes "need to be boarded for
the weekend."[1] The starkness of this diction—both stripped of a sense of
cure and imbued with connotations of business and profit—allows Bamford to cut directly, if painfully, to a core aspect of the spatial management of mental illness in contemporary American society: objects are

Social Text 148 · Vol. 39, No. 3 · September 2021
DOI 10.1215/01642472-9034418   © 2021 Duke University Press

put in "public storage," while animals are "boarded for the weekend." Even though isolation is both a cause and effect of mental struggle—as Michael J. Constantino and colleagues summarize it, "Interpersonal isolation has been implicated [in] lower well-being, greater aggression, more feelings of social rejection, more depression, and a higher likelihood of suicide attempts"[2]—we still turn to spatial confinement as a key mode of social control, from "go to your room" to imprisonment, from emigration restrictions to psych wards. As Michel Foucault notes, in a somewhat less concise manner than Bamford, "Discipline is, above all, analysis of space; it is individualization through space. . . . With the application of the discipline of medical space, and by the fact that it is possible to isolate each individual, install him in a bed, prescribe for him a regimen, etc., one is led toward an individualizing medicine."[3] Foucault argues in *Madness and Civilization* that this spatial individuation renders docile the mad or mentally ill person; it fixes the definition of madness in place by fixing the mad person in space. As he puts it, ships of fools held "fugitive" and outsider status, while hospitals "moored" madness, held it in place, "retained and maintained" it.[4] In his view, the relatively recent medicalization of the hospital—the very idea that these are places of cure—does not at all mean we have "relax[ed] the old practices of internment" but have, rather, "tightened them around the mad."[5] So why does Bamford's use of dehumanizing diction matter? Because psychiatry's capture of madness (and its attendant spatial tightening) still passes as necessarily humane and rehabilitative; even if, sometimes, such spaces do "help" individuals, they are rooted historically in punishment, control, involuntary residence, and the use of force and state power. Bamford's seemingly shocking joke—implying she is an object or an animal—is funny because, like many jokes, it speaks an uncomfortable truth: these are spaces of confinement and storage where hallmarks of the neoliberal human subject (choice, rationality, agency) are suspended.

Second, and to evince this last point, let me tell you just one of many possible stories deriving from a two-week staycation I took as a psych patient in Fredericton, New Brunswick, Canada, in 2016.[6] Two days into my sojourn, a nurse asked me if I would prefer a "male" roommate or a "female" roommate, a question seemingly based in the kind of patient-driven care that would lead us to refute Bamford's use of such startling diction. But what does spatial choice mean in the psych ward, where spatial confinement is the raison d'être? Leaving the psych ward was not an option. Neither were the following: not choosing male or female, responding with a third option (at least, having that response understood and respected), avoiding the outdated and presumptuous language of *male* and *female*, or, of course, not responding at all. Adrienne Rich's oft-quoted work on compulsory heterosexuality (and Robert McRuer's extension of it into compulsory able-bodiedness) lays the groundwork here:[7] my "choice" was triply compulsory, not least because, after I answered "Female," the nurse told me they were in fact obligated to room me with "other females" but wanted to ask anyway. Clearly, this was a pretend choice crowded in by a set of other pretend choices. The psych ward is a compulsory (or "involuntary") space in the first instance, and its gendering practices are compulsory as well—"male or female?" can become "pick your poison." (And this is not to mention the self-appointed and perhaps confused "ally" who took my weekend leave as an opportunity to walk room to room and tell the whole ward that I was "really a woman.") Yes, this staycation probably had some upsides here and there, but it still merits a bad Yelp review.

Our commonsense notion of the psychiatric ward or institution as humane depends on the production of exactly this sort of veneer of choice—in a space where few choose to go. But perhaps my own example seems exceptional rather than representative. Here, then, is a simple instance of psych ward design protocol that exemplifies the desire not to appear to confine while existing in order to confine. The Facilities Guidelines Institute (FGI), an American nonprofit organization from which no less than thirty-nine states have adopted their health care design guidelines, criticizes the punitive appearance of past designs. In a white paper, FGI authors James M. Hunt and David M. Sine give the following warning about window covers: "In the past, very heavy stainless steel screens were often installed as a safety measure. Although still used in some facilities, these screens provide a very institutional or prison-like appearance."[8] In this design formula it is not cruel or questionable to confine, but it is cruel or questionable to appear to do so. The responsibility of design, in such a case, would be to conceal, not reveal, the actual function of the space. This superficial denial of the ward's very purpose mirrors the logic of other internment designs, for instance, a pink prison cell for children introduced recently in Abingdon, England, by the Thames Valley Police.[9] While pink (Baker-Miller Pink in particular) has been lauded for its ability to reduce aggression,[10] the role of design here is to produce a literal (pink) facade of humaneness. Calming seems like a benign and generous impulse, but Foucault reminds us that making bodies docile is not neutral; it is the very exercise through which treatment—as the enforcement of a particular emotional/spatial/individual order and compliance—takes hold.[11] Calmness sounds great, sure—but compulsory calm is surely a weaponization of affect related to confinement. Yet (or, indeed), I remained very calm throughout the many times I was misgendered in the psych ward (likewise during one nurse's suggestion of prayer and another's of weight loss) because, as it is for many patients, earning permission to leave the hospital became a key motivating factor for my comportment.

With the above parables of madness's spatial confinement, I want to underline from the outset (a) that we too often mistake docility and obedience for healing, (b) that the fixity of madness in the space of the psych ward is relatively recent and not neutral, and (c) that trans people, already occupying a tenuous position (in the minds of many) vis-à-vis the concepts of humanity and sanity, bear too frequently the consequences of spatial segregation and its gender-charged norms. What, then, are the problems into which this article seeks to make its interventions? To be blunt, they are the making docile of trans madness and the rendering apolitical of the role of gender nonnormativity in conceptions of mental illness. I interpret this docility as related to four problems: (a) the confinement and fixity of madness, (b) an overemphasis on logic and rationality in mental health discourse, (c) forgetfulness of the role of sensuality in what is called "health," and (d) the presumption that mental strife and its apparent resolution are an individual rather than social or collective matter.

In response, I analyze installation art (UK artists Hannah Hull and James Leadbitter's "Madlove: A Designer Asylum") and performance art (the oeuvre of Montreal artist Coral Short) for alternatives to these four issues that together encourage us to hold gender nonconformity far from madness and madness far from body politics. What I find in the work of these collaborative artists is the following: rather than confine, these artists embark; rather than rationalize, these artists emote; rather than heal, these artists sense; and rather than individualize or individuate, these artists collect. Artworks that portray or enact (gendered) madness, weirdness, or pain in ways that queerly embark, emote, sense, and collect are, in the limited and speculative fantasy of this article, performing the public work of developing a "trans-mad" aesthetic.

Why *trans*? As I show in greater detail below, the *trans* in *trans-mad* is crucial because (a) gender nonnormativity and madness have long been mutually constitutive as categories; (b) the status of madness occupies a fraught place in trans discourse at current, as sanity still functions as a key notion through which some of us try to claim dignity, rights, and access; and (c) why not? I am trans. One of the artists whose work I analyze is nonbinary. The stakes of the social life of madness are especially high for people who face forms of social exclusion that appear under other signs and names. The psych ward is a (partly, or sometimes totally) sex-segregated space that has received scant attention relative to the question of washroom access. And, of course, when we read an article that does not mention trans people, we do not often say, "But why are cis people so central to this argument?" So why are trans people important here? Allow me to forgo the illusions of argumentation here and say: I want us to be. I wish we were. I believe, perhaps madly, that writing can be a way of hallucinating a possible life into existence. However, as I show in a slightly more argumentative register below, there can be no fulsome image of madness that does not include public gender nonconformity in the category's history and present.

Trans = Mad = Trans = Mad =

The *trans* in *trans-mad* can be read as capaciously as possible. In this, I follow the trans studies shift away from considering *trans* solely as referring to particular human subjects (to something less predetermined in its referent—to a critical operation). Unpacking Trans Studies 101 is somewhat maddening, so please allow me to cite Cáel M. Keegan's apt summary of how *trans* functions as an analytic in the field. Keegan suggests that, after Sandy Stone's influential 1987 article "The *Empire* Strikes Back: A Posttranssexual Manifesto," trans studies has

> shift[ed] the focus of inquiry from transgender objects to "trans" as an analytic for "linking the questions of space and movement . . . to other critical crossings of categorical territories" (Stryker, Currah, and Moore 12). Today transgender studies describes *trans** not as an identification, but as a force characterized by unpredictable flows across discrete forms, a "paratactic" that enacts the prepositional "with, through, of, in and across" animating vitality itself (Hayward and Weinstein 196). . . . The sticky fingers of the fronded asterisk (*) are the speculative lines of transgender's felt imaginary, sensing outward with faith to realize new contacts.[12]

Following this description of the field's shift, I can say what I do *not* mean by a trans-mad aesthetic of space: I do not mean people who are both trans and mad, or forcibly connecting transgender and madness. On the contrary, I mean to underline the dubiousness of the *both* and the *and* in the preceding sentence; the "sticky fingers" of *trans** or *trans* already have a grasp on the sticky fingers of mad/crazy. This method is also inspired by Therí Alyce Pickens, who in *Black Madness :: Mad Blackness* wants to "debunk the perception" that you don't need to say *Black madness* because *Black* presumes madness, anger, and irrationality. Similarly, to say *trans-mad* is not to collapse the words entirely but is at least to name and reconsider the perceptions (trans = mad, gender nonconformity = madness) that underlie histories of transgender and madness. The purpose of this section is then to illustrate this by referencing a few broad histories and a few telling examples. It is beyond the scope of one article, or of one person, to create an exhaustive account of trans-mad moments. No doubt readers will call to mind many other textual or historical events when reviewing my own humble selection. Please scribble them down in the margins!

Transgender's relation to madness is in hyperflux at present, owing to the ongoing assimilation of transgender to the mainstream (and, thereby, to bureaucratic genres such as health insurance). As such, in recent years, claims of "real" mental illness and antimadness messages have calcified throughout some campaigns for transgender acceptance. To get a sense of the fraught status of mental illness in transgender equality discourse, consider a 2009 poster by ILGA-Europe (the European branch of the International Lesbian, Gay, Bisexual, Trans and Intersex Association), which reads, "Transgender people are not mentally ill" at the top and "Stop the pathologisation of transgender people!" at the bottom.[13] The poster, which also expresses support for the International Trans Depathologization Network, features two white or white-passing people leaning on a desk bedecked with a psychology textbook and clipboards. A man wears a white lab coat and a stethoscope, while a woman chews on her glasses; both direct scrutinizing gazes outward at the poster's viewers. The poster specifically invokes the space of the doctor's office as the space of the pathologizing cis gaze. (Rightly so, though I note that pathologizing transgender happens everywhere, in innumerable quotidian ways—perhaps everywhere that social and political suffering is reread and rerouted as an individual medical problem.) The poster implies that mental illness is a bad thing; that being associated with mental illness somehow invalidates transgender identity and experience; and that mental illness is a fixed category that labels an observable reality that is unrelated to gender. Does this strategy appeal? Do trans people deserve better treatment if they are *not* mentally ill? Is it virtuous or victorious to escape suffering or medical regimes (or to pass as such)?

Those new to transgender discourse need to know what motivates this desire to publicly abject madness as a way to gain dignity. (These campaigns exist for good reason: people do, even if unaware, funnel cis-supremacy through psych discourses to legitimize its expression and to couch it in a rhetoric of care.) Indeed, transgender occupies an impossible position in mental health discourse: by refusing to be stigmatized as mad, trans people may obtain some dignity and agency, but only by proving we have legitimate mental conditions do resources such as hormones, surgeries, and coverage become thinkable (though not always, or often, available). I assert that this double bind derives from two related histories. First, film and television have long represented gender-crossing people as dangerously mad, as public health risks. Consider that Jame Gumb in director Jonathan Demme's *Silence of the Lambs* (1991) sews a suit of women's skin after being denied sex reassignment; that Michael Caine in Brian De Palma's *Dressed to Kill* (1980) plays a male psychiatrist *and* his own troubled patient, the murderous woman Bobbi; that Norman Bates's homicidal nature in Alfred Hitchcock's *Psycho* (1960) manifests as cross-dressing; and that characters like TV series *CSI*'s Paul Millander, the franchise's first serial killer, is a transgender man seemingly set on becoming his own late father. (Why so many mad *white* trans murderers? For Pickens, "Whiteness [carries] the presumption of ability."[14] Similarly, I wonder if what terrifies white audiences about these films is partly the corruptibility of whiteness by gender madness and partly a presumed and disturbing inclination on the part of white audiences to interpret gender-crossing characters of color as already signifying madness or emotional incapacity of a sort.)

The second history that may help us understand the depathologization strategy is the medicalization of gender-crossing that occurred with the rise of sexology. Often with fetishistic fervor, a long series of white cisgender men in psych fields have defined the protocols of our lives and care, from Magnus Hirschfeld's "transvestism" (1910), Havelock Ellis's "sexo-aesthetic inversion" (1913), Harry Benjamin's "Sex Orientation Scale" (1966), John Money's controversial and impactful notion of "gender identity" (1972) and the experiments he undertook on children, and even Toronto's Kenneth Zucker, who until 2015 championed conversion therapy as head of the Gender Identity Service at the Centre for Addiction and Mental Health.[15] It is understandable that transgender people would fight against the pathologization of our lives, if we are represented by cis people as mad murderers and if, simultaneously, the definitions, treatments, and protocols that govern our bodies are decided by a long series of white cisgender men in the psych fields (even if some had benevolent intentions).[16] None of this is to suggest that trans mental illness is "just" a bureaucratic or otherwise discursive matter. Transgender mental suffering, including my own, is visceral and high stakes. But I follow Tobin Siebers's assertion that "suffering is a signal to the self at risk"[17]—at risk of transphobia, exclusion, stigma, violence, and more—rather than a signal of a preexisting condition that lives before and beyond language, norms, and other people.

Instead of idling in an impasse—are we mad, or aren't we?—we can remember a few of the ways that madness has long been about public gender nonconformity. Consider the Greek myth of Proteus's three daughters, who refused to worship Dionysus (god of wine and fertility), which is to say, they declined his drunk orgies. As punishment, he turned them mad and let them roam the country mooing like cows and allowing their clothes to fall into disrepair—until other women follow suit. Proteus then commissioned Melampus to treat (i.e., drug?) his three daughters with hellebore to cure them, giving Melampus one of his daughters to marry, as well as part of his territory; domesticity and property moor the story and its women in place. Consider also the etymology of *hysteria*, which, as many have noted, comes from the Greek *hystera*, or "uterus."

Most famously, Plato, in the *Timaeus*, attributes hysteria to a "wandering womb," as though a woman's mad behavior were caused by "unhinged" organs.[18] As Geoffrey Chamberlain shows in his history of British obstetrics and gynecology, once "anatomical dissections had demonstrated that the uterus was actually tethered fast into the pelvis by pairs of ligaments," the narrative of women's madness did not cease to exist but, rather, shifted paradigms accordingly: "Some of the gynaecological diseases that had been considered to be due to the migration of the uterus were now attributed to the vapours."[19] (Chamberlain quotes seventeenth-century midwife Jane Sharp, who explains women's hysteria thusly: "It is most commonly the widowes disease, those who were wont to use Copulation, and are now constrained to live without it; when the seed is thus retained it corrups, and sends up filthy vapours to the brain."[20]) In each of these moments, hear an enduring message: you're crazy if you don't want to fuck men (often said or implied by precisely the man who would partake in such reparative fucking). Hear also in each of these a sense of wandering and movement: in the case of Melampus, women refusing a man's sexual advances leads to countryside madness, wandering as wildly as wombs in Plato's account, and a patriarchal drugging "fixes" their appearances, desires, and domesticities to space. (Recall Foucault's sense that the fugitive outsider status of the ship of fools was eradicated when madness became so tightly fixed to the hospital and its perfect order of individualizing space.) In just this small sample, it is clear that normative gender and sexuality are built into a variety of Western notions of sanity. Mental illness cannot be regarded as a label applied to transgender after the fact, as if we need to simply peel it off of us. Gender is, literally and metaphorically, a "fixture" of mental wellness and illness, a hook on which the meaning of sanity hangs (over us). To return to the ILGA poster: if we can understand madness and transgender as epistemological and diagnostic categories that did not develop in cultural isolation, we must acknowledge that the two cannot be held so separately.

The integral place of race in histories of madness is also, of course, robust. Consider prominent Southern physician Samuel Cartwright, who coined the term *drapetomania*—mania for running away—to describe the mental "disease" exhibited by slaves who fled captivity.[21] Or, recall the work of Jonathan Metzl, who shows in *The Protest Psychosis: How Schizophrenia Became a Black Disease* that the addition of the words *hostility* and *aggression* to diagnostic wording in the second edition of the *Diagnostic and Statistical Manual of Mental Disorders* (1968) led to a spike of schizophrenia diagnoses for Black people in civil-rights-era Michigan.[22] Closer to home for me, we could note the Sexual Sterilization Act of the Canadian province of Alberta.[23] As we can well imagine, white medical professionals deciding who qualifies as "feebleminded" or "mentally defective" is far from a racially neutral determination in the context of colonialism. As Karen Stote describes, Indigenous women "were overrepresented to the provincial Eugenics Board, and once approved for sterilization, were more likely to be subject to the procedure."[24] Some may want to hold identities far from mental illness to confer dignity or agency, but that strategy denies the ways in which the boundary between sane and insane flexes and fluctuates according to racialized and gendered notions of what is publicly good and who is authorized to make such determinations.[25]

If we take the intertwining of these social histories seriously, then we know that *trans* is never without a sense of *mad*, and vice versa. *Trans-mad*, then, is descriptive rather than additive; it is meant to remind us of the inextricability of these terms, not to putatively add one discrete experience to another. The position of this author is that to theorize madness without considering its trans or otherwise nonconforming genders would be to perpetuate the very cis-normative framework through which gender-nonconforming people are oppressed—sometimes to a point of intense mental strife.

Sense and "Madlove: The Designer Asylum"

Can we imagine spaces of mad gender beyond the doctor's office of the ILGA poster? Can we create a counterpublic that does not require "public storage" for those emotions and genders it deems excessive? More specifically, if recovering from mental strife is, at base, about feeling better, do we not need a psych ward aesthetic that takes the haptic seriously—not only as a realm requiring deep thought by designers and public health officials but also as a realm requiring aesthetic engagement? Since 2014, artists James Leadbitter (also known as "the vacuum cleaner") and Hannah Hull have undertaken a collaborative project that works to invigorate psych ward design norms by considering the haptic realm. The goal of "Madlove: A Designer Asylum" is "to create a unique space where mutual care blossoms . . . to put the treat back into treatment." This tongue-in-cheek tone—cleverly discomfiting in a manner comparable to Bamford's comedy—already introduces a new presence of sensuality in psych treatment, via the unlikely idea that it could include pleasure (a "treat"). The duo visited ten wards across the United Kingdom, as well as ones in Riga, Zurich, and Prague; did live illustrations of the group brainstorming sessions; and launched a three-month installation meant to capture the utopian psych ward and its participants (many of whom were patients at the time).[26]

It is important to note, first, that there is already a history of perceiving hospital design as crucial to healing. Between 1972 and 1981, geographer Roger Ulrich studied forty-six patients recovering from gall bladder surgery in a suburban Pennsylvania Hospital. Half had a brick wall view; half had a landscape view. The "natural setting" patients recovered quicker and took fewer drugs.[27] Thus began the booming industry of evidence-based design (EBD). Architectural critics have voiced various disagreements with Ulrich's approach, ranging from the movement's reliance on a relatively limited set of data to its excessively quantitative approach to aesthetics. As Mahbub Rashid writes, "Proponents of EBD must acknowledge that design knowledge relevant to healthcare can be found in disciplines unrelated to healthcare [and] that design knowledge does not always need empirical validation."[28] There are myriad options: we could show patients the history of madness in art; we could show patients the vast array of art brut made by mad people; we could move beyond the psych ward's use of rote art projects as a form of occupational therapy and provide more affecting art classes, and so forth. The *Behavioral Health Design Guide* by Hunt, Sine, and Kimberley N. McMurray has just a short section about "Pictures and Artwork," which dictates, "All pictures and artwork in patient-accessible areas must be given special consideration."[29] In a past edition of the guide, the photograph that accompanied this point illustrated all too clearly how humble a role is afforded to art in many a psych ward: the image shows a large cartoonish mural of two apes sitting in greenery. Nothing says "welcome to the jungle" like an ape mural in a psych ward!

In contrast, Hull and Leadbitter focus on aesthetics as an integral part of healing. The artists ask patients about preferred designs, use live illustration to facilitate the conversations, and employ installation art to communicate their findings. The desire for more meaningful ways to make art comes up often among participants. "White walls to attack with paint" or that "can be changed" are the wishes of many participants and are very different from the rote completions of crafts I remember from my occupational therapy sessions in the ward (which were still one of the best parts of the day). Art objects also come up as a source of destruction; one participant names "Fabergé eggs to smash" as a desired psych ward supply. Turning to the installation, the extent of color and ornament contrasts starkly with most contemporary medical spaces: we see deep blues, pinks, reds, yellows, and more. Varieties of texture feature here too: plush carpet, rippling curtains, stripes that draw in the eye, delicate plants, rough bricks, and so on. Again, this emphasis on the senses suggests that "feeling better" has something to do with what we, in the most literal sense, feel. One illustration in "Madlove" focuses entirely on texture: a large hand occupies the center of the drawing, and participant suggestions of what they would like to feel in psych wards surround the hand: "sand or carpet under feet," "smooth things," "clay," "facial hair," "marble sculpture," "things to fiddle with," and even "popping bubble wrap."

The space's assertion of sensuality (so different from a space that takes rationality as its aesthetic guide) extends even to the olfactory realm: in a playful twist on "smelling salts"—associated most enduringly, and tellingly, with fainting women in Victorian England[30]—the designer asylum boasts a series of scents in silver canisters, with aromas ranging from dark chocolate to thunderstorm. Another illustration lists the following words in sequence: "taste smell sound touch look," while one participant notes explicitly that current wards rely too much on visuality. In sum, the senses matter here as much as any dematerialized definition of "the mind."

In the psych wards with which I'm familiar, space is clearly demarcated: nobody is allowed to visit other patients' rooms—a community space or "dayroom" is the only shared space; other rooms are locked until sessions occur there. In Hull and Leadbitter's installation, by contrast, we see nooks and corners that undo a strict public/private binary, as if to suggest that complete visibility (that "trap" of which Foucault warns in *Discipline and Punish*) is not actually necessary for healing. Consider the "Turkish Delight" feature, an enclosure that seats several people face to face on cushioned red benches with a large rounded entrance.[31] The vibrant red of the interior contrasts with the white exterior, as if underlining the feature's creation of partially private social space. A nook atop a small set of stairs also offers a sense of privacy despite not being enclosed: pillows, books, and the size of the stoop all announce the space to visitors as a place to read or otherwise be alone. There are few straight lines or symmetrical features here (one participant's contribution to a live illustration is the sentence, "Linear is ridiculous"): the top of the "Turkish Delight" curves upward like the top of a tent, while the ceiling—lined with over a dozen white umbrellas hanging upside down—echoes these curves.

Clearly, whimsy infuses the project. This includes the rhetorical style of the project's online narratives: "Madlove is not the lunatics taking over the asylum . . . , we are proposing that we should design, build and run the asylum too." Collective force and reclamation of agency infuse this humor with serious purpose. But the "Cooling Tower" best emphasizes the stakes of this whimsy. This tall, narrow, and enclosed space plays openly with the history of psychiatric confinement: it is, in short, a padded room! Unlike padded rooms into which individuals were forced, one enters the "Cooling Tower" voluntarily and without physical restraints. The padding consists of fuchsia pillows, which are lit from above by a single suspended lightbulb. In the resultant soft pink glow, visitors/patients are welcomed to "cool off"—that is, to scream. The scream is precisely that nonrational, somatic expression of feeling that would normally cause nurses or security staff to come running in a psych ward; here, the scream is anticipated, even welcomed, in a way that makes the history of psychiatric space signify anew.

To authorities hoping for docile patients, to ward designers who favor austere medical aesthetics, and to any who would have psych patients focus on the mind in opposition to the body, "Madlove" invites us to, instead, sense.

Embark and Emote: Coral Short

I myself sense that a scream is enough to make seemingly disparate artists true allies. From the "Cooling Tower" of "Madlove," a semiprivate and individual scream space in a utopian ward, we slide along a vibrating vocal cord to the "Scream Choirs" of Montreal nonbinary performance artist Coral Short, whose large ensembles take extreme emotion into the public sphere via collaboration.[32] While advocating for concrete design changes in psychiatric space is a worthwhile project (if a very long-term one), Short's oeuvre reminds us that we can translate the sensual interventions of "Madlove" into the public sphere more immediately, if temporarily and tenuously. For Foucault, the ship of fools set madness outward on unknowable journeys—"embarkation"—while hospitals replaced this model with staying still, with "confinement," a "world of disorder, in perfect order."[33] By *embark*, I do not mean to suggest that Foucault thinks there is a preferable preconfinement spatial mode of madness to which we should or even could return. Rather, I mean to denote any breaking free of the deep belief that madness (and feeling in general) ought to, necessarily and always, be neutralized via confinement (in wards, homes, rooms, or even interior monologues).

Short's work loudly refuses any such spatial fixity. In "Scream Choir," Short choreographs choirs in public places and has them scream instead of sing. First presented for Sappyfest (Sackville, New Brunswick) and Encuentro (the biennial gathering of the Hemispheric Institute—the 2014 edition took place in Montreal), "Scream Choir" has morphed into a number of variations (Laugh Choir, Emotion Choir, and Orgasm Choir) that have appeared in Prince Edward Island (Canada), Athens, and Berlin. Short explains their purpose: "The screamers pour out emotions of anger, pain and more, in tonal yells and primal screams. This cathartic work releases pent up rage against the frustrating capitalist patriarchal machine. This sound ritual aims to be a transformative experience for both performers and audience."[34]

These screams of mad trans range, of queer pleasure, of resistance or resignation, of suffering or climaxing, are inscrutable. Screams are the ultimate onomatopoeia, only they never coalesce into sense. This is the strength of the scream for Short: it refuses to make itself legible in the usual vocabularies of the public sphere, where screams are associated with danger, and choirs are associated with polite entertainment or worship.

Short mentions that the work is "cathartic" in its "transformative" effect; an emotional shift is imagined to have happened via the corporeal—not intelligible, disembodied, or rational—experience of the scream. In a culture where variations of the talking cure still reign as primary modes of emotional relief, Short offers visceral healing: intense expressions of feelings that do not need to be understood by others but can only be created with others. Indeed, what turns a public scream from a sign of danger to a sign of performance art is the project's collaborative quality (would one person screaming in a public square be understood as art, even "weird" art, by onlookers?). Short represents healing as collective and mysterious; the pained cry and its possibility of catharsis are depicted not as individual tasks or responsibilities but as artful and cooperative disruptions.

For the 2014 Montreal incarnation of "Scream Choir," the performance site was crucial: the iconic Basilique Notre-Dame de Montréal (Notre-Dame Basilica) in Old Montreal. As noted in a piece about the safety of Montreal's heritage churches written after Notre-Dame de Paris's burning, Montreal's basilica sees 11 million visitors annually.[35] (It also has the distinction of having hosted the 1994 wedding of Quebec's, and Canada's, most famous celebrity, Céline Dion.) The basilica makes a delicious setting for "Scream Choir" because it is well known for its choral programming and its Christmas presentations of Handel's *Messiah*. The basilica is, in other words, a place of sacred music, a place where singing hinges together religion and the public sphere, a site of worship where prayer (presumably a private and spiritual activity) becomes collective, incarnate, and public. Above, I suggested that only the collective nature of "Scream Choir" makes it readable as art rather than as a sign of danger. However, definitions of art vary, of course: photos show a basilica staff member calling the police on Short's ensemble. The choir was indeed interpreted as a threat—but to what? A basilica's association with publicly beloved choral performance inverts here: queer screamers make noise without clear gods, as if to break more silences than words could break. There are a good many sensible reasons to scream when you are queer or otherwise (publicly) marginalized and good reasons to scream at or near a church in particular. Screaming has long been connected to medical approaches to emotion (Freud posits in early work that the scream is crucial to the infant's attainment of language, while Arthur Janov famously extends Freud's work in *The Primal Scream. Primal Therapy: The Cure for Neurosis*),[36] but here it becomes a different kind of madness: anger (though not exclusively that) and not a lonely one to be fixed via a private fixing of the self.

Short's work suggests that we need to learn to feel differently in public—to embark with our feelings into the public sphere and to emote. "Crying Machine," an interactive and durational piece performed at

Toronto's 2010 TRIGGER Festival suggests we need to experiment with new modes of collective suffering and emoting in order to do so. In this low-fi production, Short sits at a small table with a pile of onions, a cutting board, and a knife. Event-goers are welcomed to sit next to Short, one at a time, while Short chops onions. The obvious outcome—Short and a single other person crying together—seems both beautiful and hilarious, as the audience knows the tears are "induced" but witness a rare scene of shared public crying nonetheless. Part of the message here may be about practice, or about the performativity of emotion: do we need to push ourselves to practice public emotion or vulnerability in any manner that opens us to it? Surely public crying ought not to be a case of "fake it till you make it," but Short implies here that it is worthwhile to motivate ourselves and one another to challenge norms of public stoicism.

"Crying Machine" takes place at an art event, which would surely change the audience's sense of what is appropriate emotional behavior. By contrast, Short's work "Practicing Intimacy" moves unapologetically through a public realm: the subway system (known in Montreal as the Metro). In this work, Short ties themself to a collaborator in a way that appears to be constraining or painful; for instance, string ties Short's hair across their eyes. Undertaken as a performance for the 2008 Nuit Blanche (the Montreal edition of an all-night urban art and performance festival), "Practicing Intimacy" moved through channels of public transit look- ing quite unlike a standard public sight. What is the Metro (or the bus), however, other than a frequent occasion of practicing public intimacies? Recent debates and memes about space sharing on public transit (e.g., "man spreading") suggest that these environments are fraught precisely because of varying notions of what kinds of public intimacy are appropri- ate. What else is a public transit map other than a web that ties places and people together in odd and sometimes constraining ways? The strings wrapped around Short's face look like just such a web of tenuous and tight connections. What better place to perform a lesson about the unspoken norms of public intimacy than public transit, the very purpose of which is people, being moved, together?

Short's three projects mentioned above fight against the will to pathologize three public emotional experiences: screaming, crying, and, in a sense, oversharing. Short asks, What if these ostensibly mad acts could be modes of a trans/queer art of public emotion? So far, though, Short's projects have leaned, slightly or drastically, toward what we tend to think of as negative affects: pain, rage, crying, and constraint. In "Plush," what we could call Short's art of queer public mental health turns explicitly to experiences of comfort and relief (a step beyond the catharsis of "Scream Choir"). Between 2013 and 2015, Short stood and walked publicly in a number of cities—at events, festivals, or simply on the street—dressed head-to-toe in a suit made of stuffed animals, offering hugs to pass-ersby. In Paris, Montreal, Toronto, Hamilton (Ontario), and St. John's (Newfoundland and Labrador), Short approached or was approached by strangers both happy and reluctant, as well as enthusiastic children. The hugs (or turned-down hugs) were not always appreciated, understood, or welcomed: a photo from the Montreal performance, which took place in the Mile End neighborhood, depicts the plushy Short walking by a pub-lic gathering of Hasidim (men from the local Hasidic Jewish commu-nity)—one member is clearly pleased by the sight of Short, while another member is discernibly annoyed. The piece breaks from the stoicism of the public sphere by reinserting not only stranger intimacy but also affection, campiness, and childhood texture—an inclusion of the haptic that recalls "Madlove." The purpose of stuffed animals is, of course, to comfort via touch—and the delighted, even thrilled, looks of some of Short's huggers show us that Short brought that purpose alive.

Together, these public performances tell us that we can scream together, we can cry together, we can practice being moved together, and we can cheer each other up with whimsy or with hugs—publicly. We can— if only sometimes, and often with difficulty and danger—embark into nonmedical places and spaces to emote. Another of Short's pieces tells us what happens when we cannot (or are seldom permitted to) do these things. "Stop Beating Yourself Up" takes direct aim at everyday lan-guages of self-care and mental wellness and subverts them. It is also a rarity in Short's oeuvre: a solo performance. In this piece, performed three times between 2013 and 2015 (in Oshawa, Montreal, and Vancou-ver), Short dresses as a champion boxer, mouthpiece in place, with large, heavy gloves ready to do damage. Before an audience, Short takes aim at themself, punching themself repeatedly in a boxing style. Cameras cap-ture the action and project it on a screen. Knowing Coral Short personally and watching them do this performance (Vancouver Queer Arts Festival, 2015) was especially difficult; it was indeed hard not to yell the title of the piece directly at Short as more and more punches landed. That Short performs this as a solo piece is telling: self-flagellation is done alone, yet with a public (even if, sometimes, an imagined one that we've rebranded as our inner monologue). The harm we do to ourselves, Short's piece sug-gests, is serious and physical. Life imitated art in too real a manner fol-lowing this last iteration of "Stop Beating Yourself Up": Short gave them-self a concussion that affected their well-being for several years. "Stop Beating Yourself Up" is a comical title that mimics languages of self-improvement, but Short knows that shifting ideas of wellness and public intimacy are serious business, serious enough to stake your body on.

Short reminds us that the injuries we sustain by refuting norms of emotion, embodiment, and space can be extensive and vary drastically among us. Note, of course, that while a church staff member calls the police on Short's "Scream Choir," no guns are drawn and nobody is murdered by a police officer. As Frank Keating argues, being seen as "dangerous" may be new to white mentally ill folks, but Black men tend to become quite familiar with being interpreted as risks to public safety.[37] I praise Short's insertion of queer emotional intimacies into the public sphere, but I would be loath to imply that all subjects have the same access to the tools this requires. Obviously, public emotion is interpreted and disciplined not only through notions of mental illness and wellness but also through ideas related to race, class, gender, sexuality, and more. As Sara Ahmed reminds us, "To speak out of anger as a woman of color is to confirm your position as the cause of tension; your anger is what threatens the social bond."[38] The stakes and safety of allowing/pursuing intense public emotion vary drastically across bodies and public perceptions thereof; so too, then, must our strategies. "White woman tears," for example, do not seem to disrupt the emotional order of the public sphere but instead confirm it, often in juxtaposition to "the figure of the angry black woman."[39] I cannot presume to prescribe strategies, but I hope the ensemble nature of the artworks analyzed here points us toward the need to undertake collaborative understandings of mental health, illness, and care and to remember that none of us are the same.

Collect: Conclusion

Together, Hull and Leadbitter's "Madlove" and Coral Short's oeuvre—both based in large collaboratives—underline the possibilities of extreme emotion, madness, and suffering that are not individualized, surveilled, or pathologized in any straightforward manner. Hull, Leadbitter, and their collaborators replace Ulrich's evidence-based design with a collective design process. Like the "Madlove" installation itself, the project description critiques the individualization of mental health repeatedly: it emphasizes "mutual care," rethinks "power relations between patient and staff," and asserts that everyone, including "mental health professionals and academics," are "on the spectrum" of mental health experience. When framed as responses to ILGA-like depathologization campaigns, these artists do not so much provide a counterargument as offer generative ways forward that change the spaces of madness (led, in Short's case, by trans and queer people and, in the case of "Madlove," by mad people). In other words, "Madlove" and Short's oeuvre share undocile aesthetics that aim to make psychiatric space ("Madlove") or the mad public (Short) anything but the boring, unadorned, utilitarian, or uninspiring genre known as a "public storage" facility—to come full circle to Maria Bamford.

Given, however, that the depathologization strategy has such under-standable motivations—madness having been used in psychiatry, popular culture, and beyond as a weapon through which to harm trans people—how does one respond to earnest and well-intentioned campaigns such as the ILGA poster? To such campaigns and to trans people who would refer to them for dignity, the artists analyzed in this essay might say that to pathologize any kind of socially situated suffering (which is, of course, all suffering) is to incline us toward individual solutions, to self-betterment, rather than toward social change or political consciousness. Instead, "Madlove" and Coral Short tell us to *collect* ourselves, a word that emphasizes collaboration, implies continuation, and omits the linear vibes of *healing* or *recovery*.

A longer answer allows me to return also to my own psych ward staycation, which I discussed in the introduction as a parable of the com-pulsory "choices" of spatial confinement. The week before I was admitted to the hospital, a number of life stressors (gynecological diagnoses, mov-ing from one Canadian coast to another, starting a new job) collided with my preexisting struggles (self-medication, depression) and a number of xenophobic occurrences (at their peak, two men yelling fat-phobic slurs at me from their car, which they then slowed in order to videotape me). When I relayed this last incident to a psychiatry resident at the hospital, he responded: "Well, you *are* quite large . . . ," as if I were so deluded as to not even understand why I was harassed, as if my body were an invi-tation to the persistent harassment that would eventually play a decent role in my mental distress. A cis male nurse, similarly, looked at me and said, without any context about my life, "Well, I like to eat, too. When I'm happy, I eat; when I'm sad, I eat." Both of these professionals viewed my body as the cause and effect of my depression, not as the matter through which oppression and mistreatment found me, hurt me, and disinclined me from entering the public sphere or connecting to others. I appeal here to Jasbir Puar's notion of *debility*, a third term beyond the ability/disability binary, one that captures "the bodily injury and social exclusion brought on by economic and political factors."[40] Depathologization strategies (and the psych ward staff members I mention above) cannot account for the lived context of madness and transgender (or, for instance, of fatness) in the social world. That is, while the inextricability of transgender and mad-ness may be contingent and imagined, it is still perpetuated and reified today: trans people may not experience their gender as a source of men-tal anguish or pain (I do not), but it will almost certainly, at some point, *become one* in a world where trans people are treated terribly and denied resources, safety, homes, jobs, support, and other opportunities. To those who would "validate" transgender life by abjecting its relation to mental illness we could say, Please do not deny the lived pain and struggle of living in a world that does not want us. Or, perhaps: hang on—it's coming for you.

Just as I had nearly completed revisions for this article, I found Alexandre Baril's excellent article "Transness as Debility: Rethinking Intersections between Trans and Disabled Embodiments," which argues that "the experience of suffering linked to some of the debilitating aspects of transness should not be overlooked."[41] Indeed, just because "the discourse of suffering can be used in ableist and cisgenderist ways to further oppress disabled and trans people,"[42] this does not mean that we should accept the dubious political strategy of repressing or otherwise concealing our pain—pain that is not sui generis but is affected by, if not generated by, oppressive others, histories, and systems. In other words, we should not need to appear pain-free to "deserve" bodily change or different experiences. Moreover, to uphold a mythical pain-free trans subject as aspirational or radical is both to be bluntly ableist and to naturalize the odd fiction that cisgender life is necessarily one free of gendered pain (or gender *as* pain). This I write as someone who associates transgender with euphoria *and* with the anguish of ableism and transphobia. I expect others, with dissimilar experiences, will feel differently than I do about some of these claims. I certainly cannot speak for others; I only hope for a wider variety of trans emotions and affective narratives to become possible. May one of these be a third route between or beyond pure pathologization or depathologization because we need to insist on a position for ourselves that permits pain but does not disqualify us from life on that basis. As Baril suggests, while depathologization may seem to be about confidence and "wellness," it is often about political fear and compliance. "What are we afraid of," Baril asks, "when we refuse to listen to the distress and suffering of some trans people? Do we fear that legitimising these voices may encourage our cisgenderist societies to revive discourses denying trans people rights, access to health care and respect?"[43] The present article, as it turns out, offers some responses to these questions.

While I believe these theoretical questions play out viscerally in the lives of many, I end with a gesture toward a more obvious definition of praxis. Keeping in mind that public art is part of, and not the entirety of, a trans-mad aesthetic, I would like to ask, Can mental health collectives—a different kind of ensemble—thrive? Projects such as "gerotopias"—a kind of retirement village for aging baby boomers, also known as an AALC, or Active Adult Lifestyle Community—could, potentially, provide a model. However, as Deane Simpson points out, gerotopias' twist on the intentional communities of the 1960s and 1970s veers more toward insularity and privilege than anything else, what she describes as a "utopia of endless vacation" based on "surplus leisure time."[44] Such intentional communities could focus on mutual care, but Simpson suggests they are currently engaged in something closer to "urban and social escapism."[45] Short's embarkation into the general public sphere—not out of it—suggests the opposite approach. I end with this gesture toward collective care and action not because I feel virtuous about it, or even particularly capable of it. On the contrary, this is what I aim to do more, after years of experiencing the effects of isolation as well as, inversely, the effects of virulent, public transphobia and fatphobia. But barriers to mutual care spaces already exist. In their case study of Toronto, Chava Finkler and Jill L. Grant explain that zoning bylaws mandate strict minimum distances between group homes for psychiatric survivors, thereby making enclaves impossible.[46] Safety is one ostensible reason for this. (Safety for whom?) Safety is also the guiding principle of McMurray, Hunt, and Sine's protocols for psych space design. Images in their *Behavioral Health Design Guide*, for example, show a dot marking every single thing in a psych ward room that psych patients could use to hurt themselves: an outlet, a blanket, a wall—almost anything. Where in these common approaches to mental health and safety do we consider that *others* hurt mentally ill people? Could we draw an FGI diagram of the psych ward and mark it with everywhere trans people have been hurt by staff and patients or by a policy or design? Can we imagine a similar diagram of a public street, square, washroom, or shelter? For me, art and performance are vital ways to respond and endure, especially since conceptions of space and architecture infuse our every thought of mental illness—from stability through breakdown to collapse. If we want to push the limits of the liberal imagination beyond the provision of a gender-neutral washroom in a psychiatric lockdown, we need trans-mad artists and thinkers to design, disrupt, and lead such spaces, in addition to sometimes convalescing in them. We need to acknowledge the debility of the trans-mad subject rather than purely reject or affirm transgender as a species of psychiatric disorder. We need to insist on a public sphere into which one can embark in order to sense, emote, and collect one another and ourselves. We have been doing it for a long time—psych professionals and designers may have some catching up to do. But if you've made it to the end of this article, you are on your way—somewhere.

Lucas Crawford is associate professor of English at the University of Alberta (Augustana Faculty). Lucas's most recent book is *Belated Bris of the Brainsick* (2019), which won the J. M. Abraham Prize as the best poetry collection published in Atlantic Canada that year.

Notes

I offer very kind thanks to Jeanne Vaccaro and Joan Lubin for their steadfast support and their generosity with my work. Thank you to the anonymous peer reviewers and to the staff of *Social Text*. This work was first presented at "Future Genders," the 2018 Max Wasserman Forum on Contemporary Art at MIT. Kind thanks to the organizers of that event, to fellow presenters, and to audience members.

1. Bamford, *Old Baby*, 36:30–37:24.
2. Constantino et al., "Existential Isolation as a Correlate of Clinical Distress," 389.
3. Foucault, "Incorporation of the Hospital into Modern Technology," 151.
4. Foucault, *Madness and Civilization*, 31.
5. Foucault, *Mental Illness and Psychology*, 70.
6. Even my mirroring of Bamford's diction above relies on the disjunction between our sense of a vacation as chosen and a hospitalization as compelled.
7. Rich, "Compulsory Heterosexuality and Lesbian Existence"; McRuer, *Crip Theory*.
8. Hunt and Sine, *Common Mistakes in Designing Psychiatric Hospitals*, 13.
9. BBC News, "Abingdon Police Open 'Calming' Pink Cell for Children."
10. St. Clair, *Secret Lives of Colour*, 118–19; Schauss, "Tranquilizing Effect of Color."
11. Tobin Siebers argues that Foucault aligns the predocile body with strength and ability and the docile body with weakness and disability: "The docile body begins to resemble disability, and it is not meant as a term of celebration" (*Disability Theory*, 58). I contend the opposite: that what Foucault calls docility aligns with what many define as the able body (e.g., the effective soldier). Siebers points out the mournful tone Foucault uses when discussing disciplined bodies, but the latter is not mourning the disablement of the docile body as much as his sense of the docile body's ability put to work in the name of state power.
12. Keegan, *Lana and Lilly Wachowski*, 4.
13. ILGA-Europe, "Transgender People Are Not Mentally Ill."
14. Pickens, *Black Madness*, 7.
15. Stryker, *Transgender History*, 31–58; Goldie, *The Man Who Invented Gender*; Ubelacker, "CAMH to 'Wind Down.'"
16. I agree with Susan Stryker that many of these cis men were advocates who sought to support trans people in some way. While the suffering these practitioners sought to alleviate was personal and visceral, it does not follow that its origins were necessarily individual/medical rather than social, affective, aesthetic, and so on. This is merely to underline that these advocates' works also played a role in the still-current control of nonnormative gender by psychiatric gatekeepers. My point is simply that while these men helped things progress, things could have progressed otherwise.
17. Siebers, *Disability Theory*, 20.
18. Gilman et al., *Hysteria beyond Freud*.
19. Chamberlain, *From Witchcraft to Wisdom*, 60.
20. Chamberlain, *From Witchcraft to Wisdom*, 60.
21. Willoughby, "Running Away from Drapetomania."
22. Metzl, *Protest Psychosis*.
23. The territory of the province of Alberta is covered by Treaty 6 (1876), Treaty 7 (1877), and Treaty 8 (1899), which were signed by the Canadian Crown and Indigenous nations—mainly, but not exclusively, Cree, Assiniboine, Ojibwa (Treaty 6), Blackfoot (Treaty 7), and the First Nations of the Lesser Slave Lake area (includ-

ing the Dane-zaa, Cree, and Denesuline people). To learn about Alberta's 1928 Sexual Sterilization Act and other eugenic legislations, see Wilson, "Eugenics Archive."

24. Stote, "Coercive Sterilization of Aboriginal Women in Canada," 120.

25. I do not presume to know or to decide how race should or could fit into the rubric I propose here, except to say that we ought to remember that *whiteness* is not a modifier to *cis* or *sane* but, rather, a constitutive element of these categories.

26. Hull and Leadbitter, "Madlove."

27. Ulrich, "View through a Window," 420–21.

28. Rashid, "Question of Knowledge," 101.

29. McMurray, Hunt, and Sine, *Behavioral Health Design Guide*, 32. Note: Before the FGI published the paper, the National Association of Psychiatric Health Systems did so (2003–2014). Note also that two of the authors are part owners of the current publisher of this white paper, Behavioral Health Facility Consulting. The FGI still offers this text as a downloadable file in its "Beyond Fundamentals" online library.

30. McCrory, "Smelling Salts."

31. I want to flag the name and design of the "Turkish Delight" feature as potentially appropriative or otherwise misguided, depending perhaps on who suggested drawing from this design history and for what purpose.

32. Coral Short, "Coral Short."

33. Foucault, *Madness and Civilization*, 32.

34. Coral Short, "Scream Choir," caption.

35. Curtis, "Notre-Dame de Paris Fire."

36. Freud, "Project for a Scientific Psychology"; Scheehan, "Reading of an Ethics of Psychoanalysis"; Janov, *Primal Scream*.

37. Keating, "Fear, Black People, and Mental Illness."

38. Ahmed, *Promise of Happiness*, 67.

39. Accapadi, "When White Women Cry," 208; Hamad, *White Tears / Brown Scars*; Hamad, "How White Women Use Strategic Tears"; Ahmed, *Promise of Happiness*, 68.

40. Puar, *Right to Maim*.

41. Baril, "Transness as Debility," 68.

42. Baril, "Transness as Debility," 70.

43. Baril, "Transness as Debility," 70.

44. Simpson, "Gerotopias," 356, 359.

45. Simpson, "Gerotopias," 362.

46. Finkler and Grant, "Minimum Separation Distance Bylaws."

References

Accapadi, Mamta Motwani. "When White Women Cry: How White Women's Tears Oppress Women of Colour." *College Student Affairs Journal* 26, no. 2 (2007): 208–15.

Ahmed, Sara. *The Promise of Happiness*. Durham, NC: Duke University Press, 2010.

Bamford, Maria. *Old Baby*. Comedy special. Directed by Jessica Yu. Los Gatos, CA: Netflix, 2017.

Baril, Alexandre. "Transness as Debility: Rethinking Intersections between Trans and Disabled Embodiments." *Feminist Review*, no. 111 (2015): 59–74.

BBC News. "Abingdon Police Open 'Calming' Pink Cell for Children." August 1, 2018. www.bbc.com/news/uk-england-oxfordshire-45037919.

Chamberlain, Geoffrey. *From Witchcraft to Wisdom: A History of Obstetrics and Gynaecology in the British Isles.* Cambridge: Royal College of Obstetricians and Gynaecologists, 2007.

Constantino, Michael J., Robert K. Sommer, Brien J. Goodwin, Alice E. Coyne, and Elizabeth C. Pinel. "Existential Isolation as a Correlate of Clinical Distress, Beliefs about Psychotherapy, and Experiences with Mental Health Treatment." *Journal of Psychotherapy Integration* 29, no. 4 (2019): 389–99.

Curtis, Christopher. "Notre-Dame de Paris Fire: How Safe Are Montreal's Heritage Churches?" *Montreal Gazette*, April 16, 2019. montrealgazette.com/news/local-news/notre-dame-de-paris-fire-how-safe- are-montreals-heritage-churches.

Finkler, Chava, and Jill L. Grant. "Minimum Separation Distance Bylaws for Group Homes: The Negative Side of Planning Regulation." *Canadian Journal of Urban Research* 20, no. 1 (2011): 33–56.

Foucault, Michel. "The Incorporation of the Hospital into Modern Technology." In *Space, Knowledge, and Power: Foucault and Geography*, edited by Jeremy W. Crampton and Stuart Elden, translated by Stuart Elden, William J. King, and Edgar Knowlton Jr., 141–51. Burlington, VT: Ashgate, 2007.

Foucault, Michel. *Madness and Civilization: A History of Insanity in the Age of Reason.* Translated by Richard Howard. New York: Routledge, 2005.

Foucault, Michel. *Mental Illness and Psychology.* Translated by Alan Sheridan. Berkeley: University of California Press, 1987.

Freud, Sigmund. "A Project for a Scientific Psychology." In *The Standard Edition of the Complete Psychological Works of Sigmund Freud*, edited and translated by James Strachey, 1:283–387. New York: Vintage Classics, 2001.

Gilman, Sander L., Helen King, Roy Porter, G. S. Roussseau, and Elaine Showalter. *Hysteria beyond Freud.* Berkeley: University of California Press, 1993.

Goldie, Terry. *The Man Who Invented Gender: Engaging the Ideas of John Money.* Vancouver: UBC Press, 2014.

Hamad, Ruby. "How White Women Use Strategic Tears to Silence Women of Colour." *Guardian*, May 7, 2018. www.theguardian.com/commentisfree/2018/may/08/how- white-women-use-strategic-tears-to-avoid-accountability.

Hamad, Ruby. *White Tears / Brown Scars.* Melbourne: Melbourne University Press, 2019.

Hull, Hannah, and James Leadbitter (the vacuum cleaner). "Madlove: A Designer Asylum." www.madlove.org.uk (accessed October 1, 2018).

Hunt, James M., and David M. Sine. *Common Mistakes in Designing Psychiatric Hospitals: An Update.* Facilities Guidelines Institute, May 2015. www.fgiguidelines.org/wp-content/uploads/2018/11/FGI_CommonMistakesPsychiatricHospitals1505.pdf.

ILGA-Europe. "Transgender People Are Not Mentally Ill." Online poster, December 2009. www.ilga-europe.org/resources/ilga-europe-reports-and-other-materials/two-posters-rights-trans-people-december-2009.

Janov, Arthur. *The Primal Scream. Primal Therapy: The Cure for Neurosis.* London: Abacus, 1977.

Keating, Frank. "Fear, Black People, and Mental Illness: A Vicious Circle?" *Health and Social Care in the Community* 12, no. 5 (2004): 439–47.

Keegan, Cáel M. *Lana and Lilly Wachowski: Sensing Transgender.* Chicago: University of Illinois Press, 2018.

McCrory, Paul. "Smelling Salts." *British Journal of Sports Medicine* 40, no. 8 (2006): 659–60.

McMurray, Kimberley N., James M. Hunt, and David M. Sine. *Behavioral Health*

Design Guide. Tuscaloosa, AL: Behavioral Health Facility Consulting, 2020. www.bhfcllc.com/design-guide/.

McRuer, Robert. *Crip Theory: Cultural Signs of Queerness and Disability*. New York: NYU Press, 2006.

Metzl, Jonathan. *The Protest Psychosis: How Schizophrenia Became a Black Disease*. Boston: Beacon, 2011.

Pickens, Theri Alyce. *Black Madness :: Mad Blackness*. Durham, NC: Duke University Press, 2019.

Puar, Jasbir. *The Right to Maim: Debility, Capacity, Disability*. Durham, NC: Duke University Press, 2017.

Rashid, Mahbub. "The Question of Knowledge in Evidence-Based Design for Healthcare Facilities: Limitations and Suggestions." *HERD: Health Environments Research and Design* 6, no. 4 (2013): 101–26.

Rich, Adrienne. "Compulsory Heterosexuality and Lesbian Existence." *Signs* 5, no. 4 (1980): 631–60. doi.org/10.1086/493756.

Schauss, Alexander G. "Tranquilizing Effect of Color Reduces Aggressive Behavior and Potential Violence." *Journal of Orthomolecular Psychiatry* 8, no. 4 (1979): 218–20.

Scheehan, Helen. "A Reading of an Ethics of Psychoanalysis from Freud's Formulation of *Das Ding* in the 'Project for a Scientific Psychology.'" In *The Prepsychoanalytic Writings of Sigmund Freud*, edited by Filip Geeradyn and Gertrudis van de Vijver, 181–89. London: Karnac, 2002.

Short, Coral. "Coral Short." www.coralshort.com (accessed October 1, 2018).

Short, Coral. "Scream Choir." YouTube, July 22, 2014. www.youtube.com/watch ?v=1vYlZd1F2tc.

Siebers, Tobin. *Disability Theory*. Ann Arbor: University of Michigan Press, 2008.

Simpson, Deane. "Gerotopias." In *Imperfect Health: The Medicalization of Architecture*, edited by Giovanna Borasi and Mirko Zardini, 351–64. Montreal: Canadian Centre for Architecture and Lars Muller.

St. Clair, Kassie. *The Secret Lives of Colour*. London: John Murray, 2016.

Stote, Karen. "The Coercive Sterilization of Aboriginal Women in Canada." *American Indian Culture and Research* 36, no. 3 (2012): 117–50.

Stryker, Susan. *Transgender History*. New York: Seal, 2008.

Ubelacker, Sheryl. "CAMH to 'Wind Down' Controversial Gender Identity Clinic Services." *Globe and Mail*, December 15, 2015. www.theglobeandmail.com/news /toronto/camh-to-wind-down-controversial-gender-identity-clinic-services /article27766580/.

Ulrich, Roger. "View through a Window May Influence Recovery from Surgery." *Science* 224, no. 4647 (1984): 420–21. doi.org/10.1126/science.6143402.

Willoughby, Christopher D. E. "Running Away from Drapetomania: Samuel A. Cartwright, Medicine, and Race in the Antebellum South." *Journal of Southern History* 84, no. 3 (2018): 579–614.

Wilson, Robert R., dir. *The Eugenics Archive*. eugenicsarchive.ca (accessed September 15, 2021).

Cripping the Welfare Queen

The Radical Potential of Disability Politics

Jina B. Kim

Over the past several decades, the mythical figure of the welfare queen has occupied a key space in the US national imaginary. Presaged by Senator Daniel Patrick Moynihan's (D-NY) 1965 report on Black matriarchal households and popularized during Ronald Reagan's 1976 bid for the Republican presidential nomination, the welfare queen offered a story of racialized mothering that would soon become the nation's primary narrative of public dependency. Reagan's depiction of a spendthrift from Chicago's South Side who posed as a mother of fourteen to obtain state benefits inaugurated a discourse of policy reform that would breed slogans like George H. W. Bush's "cross-generational dependency," the commonly invoked "welfare as a way of life," and the Clinton administration's "end of welfare as we know it." This narrative of dependency, anchored by ever-present mythologies of pathological Black motherhood, has vitally shaped the ongoing regime of state divestment, whose intensification of material and social inequality we see fully in our contemporary moment. It represents a key tactic in a persistent history of state-sanctioned assaults on racialized maternity, which range from the breaking of kinship ties along the Black Atlantic to the punitive surveillance of state foster care practices.

Following the propagation of this mythology by Reagan and others, feminist writers, scholars, and activists claimed the welfare mother as a generative site for Black feminist and feminist-of-color thought. In Cathy Cohen's pathbreaking 1997 essay "Punks, Bulldaggers, and Welfare Queens," the "non-normative and marginal" position of the welfare queen becomes one of the centers around which a radical queer politics might take shape.[1] Sapphire's novel *Push* (1996), published the same year

Social Text 148 · Vol. 39, No. 3 · September 2021
DOI 10.1215/01642472-9034390 © 2021 Duke University Press

as major US welfare reform, mobilizes the figure of the welfare queen to map the purposeful failures of public support systems in a Reagan-era New York City. *Push*, too, underscores the radical potential for "progressive transformative coalition work" among the groups most antagonized by antiwelfare policy: racialized, low-income, and disabled populations.[2]

The relationship between the protagonist, sixteen-year-old Claireece "Precious" Jones, and her disabled infant daughter rehearses the possibility of such an alliance. In introducing her daughter, Precious states: "[My mother] don't love me. I wonder how she could love Little Mongo (thas my daughter). . . . What it is short for is Mongoloid Down Sinder, which is what she is; sometimes what I feel I is."[3] For scholars of disability studies, this passage may seem a strange place to locate political affinity, as it reduces the baby daughter to a diagnostic category.[4] But in naming her daughter "Little Mongo," an affectionate diminutive, Precious renders the language of diagnosis strange, redirecting it from its intended function of pathology to one of coalition and kinship. "Mongoloid Down Sinder" names what her daughter is and also what Precious sometimes feels she is. As I demonstrate in this essay, the unexpected affinity between Precious as welfare mother and her disabled baby daughter is not incidental. Rather, it reflects how ableist reasoning anchors antiwelfare rhetoric, casting entire categories of people as undeserving of public support. Though the language of reform may devalue Precious and Mongo by casting them both as dependent on public resources, writers like Sapphire demonstrate how dependency might function as an unexpected axis of affinity between groups framed as drains on the state.

This essay outlines the contours of this coalitional axis. Drawing together feminist- and queer-of-color critique with disability theory, it offers a literary-cultural reframing of racialized mothering considering critical discourses of disability. Whereas antiwelfare policy often casts independence and self-ownership as national ideals, my analysis of the welfare mother elaborates a version of disability and feminist-of-color analysis that not only takes dependency as a given but also mines the term for its transformative potential. Rather than a negative property ascribed to certain segments of the population, here *dependency* describes a relationship articulated across all subjects and the support systems in which they are embedded—a recurring social and material bond vital to survival.

To imagine the welfare mother as a site for recuperating and reenvisioning dependency, I draw on the "ruptural possibilities" of minority literary forms, to use Roderick A. Ferguson's coinage,[5] and place Sapphire's *Push* in conversation with Jesmyn Ward's acclaimed novel *Salvage the Bones* (2011). Both novels depict young Black mothers grappling with the disabling context of public infrastructural abandonment, in which the basic support systems for maintaining life—public schools, hospitals, housing, social services—have become increasingly compromised. As such, these novels enable an elaboration of a critical disability politic centered on welfare queen mythology and its attendant structures of state neglect, one that identifies, contests, and overwrites the punitive logics of public resource distribution. This disability politic, which I term *crip-of-color critique*, foregrounds the critical purchase of disability for Black feminist and feminist-of-color theories of gendered and sexual state regulation and in turn ushers considerations of racialized reproduction and state violence to the forefront of critical disability analysis.

Toward a Crip-of-Color Critique

How might disability studies shift if it took up the welfare queen as a central site of inquiry? And in turn, how might a disability analysis highlight the little-acknowledged ways that discourses of *inability* have shaped the figure of the welfare queen and imbued her with rhetorical power? The welfare queen functions as perhaps the definitive disability narrative of late capitalism: a cautionary tale of state dependency that enabled the reallocation of public resources toward a global elite. Yet disability remains overlooked in scholarly considerations of this figure, even as Black feminist critics like Cathy Cohen, Dorothy Roberts, Wahneema Lubiano, and Alexis Pauline Gumbs have thoroughly outlined the gendered, raced, classed, and queer dimensions of her narrative. The welfare queen, however, became legible as a public figure largely through ableist language and reasoning: she is defined necessarily as a pathological mother, a social aberrance to be rehabilitated through workfare programs. Through her alleged inability to mother, work, or re/produce in accordance with social norms, articulated through the charge of her dependency on state resources, she furnished a useful "cover story" for global capitalism to propagate itself through the dismantling of social safety nets.[6]

Alongside the rhetorical mainstays of anti-Blackness and misogyny, the language of disability, pathology, and disease wrote the welfare queen into public legibility. According to Sanford F. Schram, the 1996 Personal Responsibility and Work Opportunity Reconciliation Act (a bill widely regarded as major US welfare reform) contributed considerably to the "medicalization" of welfare, as the act "helped accelerate the tendency to construct welfare dependency as an illness, thereby transforming welfare reform into a set of therapeutic interventions designed to cure people of a malady."[7] In other words, the dominant ideology of welfare dependency framed the need for public assistance as a disability in itself, one subject to state management and cure. And as both Linda Singer and Alexis Pauline Gumbs have argued, the Reagan-era discourse around racialized reproduction framed Black teenage motherhood as an epidemic, one that justified the "wars on poverty and drugs that combined to situate disease and enmity in the bodies of poor women."[8] The Black mother as disease, Gumbs elaborates, "[posed] a threat on privileged populations through tax burdens, crime, and the general erosion of quality of life," representing a path of infection that moved from "oppressed" sites to privileged ones.[9] Framed as both epidemic and threat, the narrative of racialized reproduction positioned poor Black mothers as disabling to the nation writ large.

Given the centrality of disability to antiwelfare mythology, I view the welfare queen as a key figure for bridging disability and feminist-of-color politics, transforming them through the mutual engagement of crip-of-color critique. At once a critical methodology, coalitional practice, and epistemological project, a crip-of-color critique attends to "the systematic relationship among forms of domination," recognizing ableism as one vector operating alongside and through other structures of oppression.[10] Following disability justice activist Patricia Berne, crip-of-color critique contends that we can understand ableism only by "grasping its interrelations with heteropatriarchy, white supremacy, colonialism, and capitalism."[11] In assessing these interrelations, a crip-of-color critique further identifies possible axes of solidarity across lineages of liberatory thought, in which the ableist logic of welfare reform offers—perhaps counterintuitively—a conduit toward political affinity and consolidation. This framework thus envisions an explicitly intersectional disability politics attuned to regulatory regimes of power, that is, how state-sanctioned and extralegal systems of domination interlock to circumscribe, police, and exploit racialized and low-income lives. Additionally, it foregrounds the strategies and responses of writers, artists, activists, and intellectuals in the face of racialized regimes of disablement.

As a critical methodology, a crip-of-color critique examines how the language of disability undergirds the ongoing erosion of public resources alongside other forms of state-sanctioned violence.[12] Disability scholars have termed this form of analysis *cripping*, a reading practice analogous to queering that "[spins] mainstream representations or practices to reveal able-bodied assumptions and exclusionary effects."[13] To be clear, cripping does not necessitate looking for diagnostic evidence of disability in a text, nor does it prioritize the positive representation of identifiably disabled characters. Rather, it uses disability as a lens for reading across literary and cultural works, through which the critic pays particular attention to how "able-bodied assumptions" inform the text at hand. Indeed, cripping can explain how a text furthers a critical disability ethos even if no disabled characters are present at all. To "crip" the welfare queen, then, does not necessitate labeling her as disabled. Rather, cripping underscores how ableist ideologies around dependency, reproduction, and labor give her story narrative power.

In "Enabling Whom? Critical Disability Studies Now," Julie Avril Minich speaks to the political necessity of shifting from a disability studies defined through its objects of inquiry to one determined by its "method of analysis," suggesting that such a shift would expand the scope of disability critique beyond its frequently single-issue focus. For Minich, disability as methodology "involves scrutinizing not bodily or mental impairments" but the "normative ideologies" that "define particular attributes as impairments" and that disproportionately concentrate disability in vulnerable populations. Embracing disability as methodology, then, would further connect the field to questions of race, power, and redistribution and, in so doing, "recommit [disability studies] to its origins in social justice work."[14] Notably for Minich, this recommitment to origins involves not only the US disability rights movement, often credited as the catalyst for disability studies, but also any and all movements that aim to liberate those with pathologized bodies and minds. In this way, disability as methodology also functions to connect liberatory movements and intellectual genealogies that may initially bear little relation to one another but whose shared resonances generate potential modes of thinking, living, and being in excess of normative ideologies.

In addition to cripping the logic of welfare reform and its "able-bodied assumptions," a crip-of-color critique also examines how the language and theory of disability intervene into dominant understandings of dependency. It takes seriously the assertion, forwarded by Nancy Fraser and Linda Gordon in "A Genealogy of Dependency," that an "adequate response" to welfare reform and state divestment "would need to question our received valuations and definitions of dependence in order to allow new, emancipatory social visions to emerge."[15] As such, a crip-of-color framework responds to dependency's pejorative usages in antiwelfare rhetoric but also advances a less derogatory definition: dependency as a value-free relationship in which someone relies on someone or something else for support. This relationship to others is not inherently stigmatized but, rather, to borrow a phrase from disability justice activist Eli Clare, "as common as morning coffee."[16] Further, drawing from feminist and disability thought, crip-of-color critique centralizes the concept of *interdependency*, a term that broadly describes a condition of shared dependence, an ecology of dependent relations, in which dependency can also be considered in terms of its mutualistic and symbiotic properties.[17] As disability justice activist Mia Mingus wrote, "Interdependency is both 'you and I' and 'we.' It is solidarity, in the best sense of the word. . . . Because the truth is: we need each other."[18] The relationship between dependency and interdependency, then, is one of recuperation: interdependency allows us to understand dependency beyond the single register of pathology and, further, prompts us to recognize the webs of support that enable us to live.

By connecting disability and feminist/queer-of-color politics across the shared resonance of inter/dependency, a crip-of-color critique functions not only as a critical methodology but also as a coalitional practice. Its emphasis on dependency as a post-civil-rights discourse that moves across categories of race, gender, and sexuality—as well as its critique of the normative ideology of independence—thus attends to, in the words of Grace Kyungwon Hong and Roderick A. Ferguson, the emergent ways that "particular populations are rendered vulnerable to processes of death and devaluation over and against other populations."[19] Hong and Ferguson speak to the urgency of developing cross-categorical analytics that "profoundly question nationalist and identitarian modes of political organization and craft alternate understandings of subjectivity, collectivity and power," particularly given the changing terrain of race and nation in the afterlives of decolonization and civil rights.[20] Single-issue frameworks built on presumed similarity cannot attend to the ostensibly colorblind language of dependency that distinguishes deserving populations from those "undeserving" of state support. In centering discourses of dependency in its analysis, a crip-of-color critique thus enables the exploration of "crip affinity," as disability scholar Lezlie Frye puts it, between disability politics and the targeted populations of welfare reform.[21]

Yet, as Frye contends, this affinity remains underexplored in disability studies because of the prominence of a rights-based framework in much first-wave disability scholarship. Informed by the 1990 passage of the Americans with Disabilities Act, the first comprehensive civil rights law for people with disabilities, this initial wave of scholarship favored a framework that posited disability as a minority identity (akin to race, sexuality, gender, etc.) to which legal rights could accrue. In so doing, this framework moved disability away from the province of medical authority and toward the realm of accommodation, social critique, and resistance. While a necessary shift, such platforms are nonetheless limited in their theorizations of disability beyond, as Michael Davidson puts it, "a Western, state-centered model that assumes values of individual rights and equality guaranteed by legal contract."[22] Further, as Dean Spade and others have argued, rights-based models implicitly frame the nation-state as a haven of protection, disregarding those populations regularly subject to state violence.[23] Some supporters of the Americans with Disabilities Act, in fact, colluded with the conservative logics of welfare reform by posing the legislation as vital to weaning disabled citizens off public assistance and sending them into the workforce.[24]

Departing from rights-based paradigms, feminist disability scholars such as Frye, Minich, Nirmala Erevelles, Jasbir Puar, and Liat Ben-Moshe have begun to examine disability's entanglements with the mechanisms of racialized state violence. A crip-of-color critique aligns itself with this emergent wave of scholarship, which theorizes disability "in terms of precarious populations" rather than those fortunate enough to access legal rights.[25] Following Frye, Minich, Erevelles, Puar, and others, it pays attention to how the state itself disables populations en masse through group-differentiated processes of resource deprivation and ableist rhetorics of dependency that frame racialized, feminized, impoverished, and disabled populations as drains on the public. In other words, it argues for a disability politics that understands the state as itself a racial-gendered apparatus of mass disablement. Following this, a crip-of-color critique underscores how the phantom of the welfare queen, alongside other bogeymen of reform (e.g., the undocumented immigrant), provides the narrative support for an ideology and praxis of resource austerity, in which the looming threat of parasitic others enables divestment in public services. In so doing, it emphasizes the close relationship between an ableist ideology of scarcity as emblematized by the welfare mother and the widespread dismantling of public infrastructure intended to support the nation's most vulnerable.

To clarify this relationship, which threads together deviant mothering, disability, narratives of scarcity, and infrastructural erosion, I now return to Sapphire's *Push*. As Michelle Jarman has noted, the novel's protagonist is "[haunted] by disability," as she must navigate the conjoined forces of "poverty, sexual abuse, illiteracy . . . , HIV, and having a daughter with Down Syndrome."[26] Precious is the product of relentless abuse; twice raped and impregnated by her father, tormented daily by her mother, and warehoused by educational and social services, she amplifies the violence of patriarchy, white supremacy, and state neglect besieging Black urban communities. And as a crip-of-color critique highlights, *Push* entangles disability with the mechanisms of state violence specific to Reagan-era reform: insufficient public infrastructures, state agencies, and municipal services that allegedly aim to offer state support but in fact work to reproduce social and material violence.

Sapphire's novel invites an intimacy with state infrastructure that functions, in the words of Aliyyah Abdur-Rahman, as the novel's "dramatic core." The prominence of "sites of public service: public schools, welfare offices, shelters, hospitals and the like" provokes a readerly attention to state infrastructure that highlights relations of support—the key maneuver of crip-of-color critique.[27] A crip-of-color critique, then, operates primarily through an infrastructural hermeneutic: a reading practice that underscores the often unnoticed networks of assistance—roads, pipes, wires, and labor networks—that coordinate contemporary life, as well as the aesthetics of support and inter/dependency unfolding across feminist-of-color literary and cultural production. At its most basic level, *infrastructure* refers to the "equipment, facilities, services, and supporting structures needed for a city's or region's functioning."[28] On a more abstract level, it can also refer to public services, such as schools, welfare assistance, and health care, and invoke informal networks that distribute life-sustaining resources in the absence of formal state support. Either way, infrastructure often eludes our attention; as the editors of the *Modern Fiction Studies* special issue on infrastructuralism put it, "Infrastructure is supposed to go unnoticed when it works."[29] Aesthetic works that then induce "infrastructural avowal," in the words of performance scholar Shannon Jackson, thus demand "an acknowledgement of the interdependent systems of support that sustain human beings": systems of support that frequently go disregarded yet remain vital to collective survival.[30] But infrastructure, too, does not just reference the systems that sustain human life. It also calls to mind the uneven distribution of material resources, in which systems of resource provision optimize life for some while conscripting others to death and disablement.

The plot of *Push* details its teenage protagonist's harrowing journey through Harlem's educational and social welfare systems, highlighting the purposeful failures of public infrastructure and state regulatory agencies at the height of the Reagan era. It opens with a censorious account of New York's public educational system, which constitutes the initial framework through which readers come to know Precious's world: "I was left back when I was twelve because I had a baby for my fahver. That was in 1983. I was out of school for a year. This gonna be my second baby. My daughter got Down Sinder. She's retarded. I had got left back in the second grade, too, when I was seven, 'cause I couldn't read (and I still peed on myself)."[31] These opening lines document the perpetuation of abuse by a system that magnifies patriarchal violence, as well as Precious's apt assessment of an educational ethos more committed to punishment than care.

As a literacy narrative, *Push* is organized around Precious's acquisition of reading and writing skills despite her subpar public education, foregrounding both the ineffective state institutions that create illiteracy in underresourced communities and the informal support systems that arise to address unmet needs. Its narrative arc details the protagonist developing new literacies from her engagement with the actively disabling infrastructures of New York's Harlem, as well as the self-actualizing, "humane, [and] fail-safe communal infrastructures" of Each One Teach One, a community-based adult learning center lead by Black lesbian poet Ms. Rain.[32] Yet, while *Push* condemns the brutality of state institutions, the novel's adoption of the literacy bildungsroman, which imposes on its protagonist a developmental journey of progress, underscores some of its limitations as a site of radical disability politics. The bildungsroman genre implicitly frames Precious as a character in need of improvement, when in fact she is already a subject of knowledge prior to her acquisition of literacy. As documented in the novel's opening lines and in her reflections on her mother-daughter relationship, Precious not only is attentive to infrastructural violence but also can identify unexpected alliances with other groups similarly under the thumb of state regulation.

Indeed, the "crip affinity" between Precious and her disabled baby daughter is further explored through the novel's expansive infrastructural tableau.[33] Precious's school, for instance, is likened to the horrific state institutions that warehouse disabled people. Just as Precious must attend a school that prioritizes punishment over education, so Mongo, her disabled daughter, is kept in a "retard house" where "she lay on floor in pee clothes."[34] By paralleling Precious's life experience with Mongo's, *Push* highlights how, to quote Cynthia Wu and Jennifer C. James, the "social, political, and cultural practices" of resource erosion work to "[keep] seemingly different groups of people in strikingly similar marginalized positions."[35] In Sapphire's novel, state institutions themselves practice the work of bad mothering, insofar as they reproduce a world incompatible with Black, disabled, and impoverished life.

Push thus renders evident the relationship of disability to antiwelfare rhetoric, as well as the potential for a critical disability politic to intervene into that rhetoric's operative logics. In terms of disability, it identifies eroding public supports as the cause, rather than the result, of the cultural pathology decried by welfare reformists.[36] Precious's illiteracy and familial trauma are facilitated by inadequate public services, which subsequently foreclose access to social mobility. The dwindling public resources on which Precious depends produce the signs of inability that then transform into the mythology of the welfare queen. In this way, the novel offers a reversal of the punitive discourse of public dependency that distinguishes between deserving and undeserving subjects. Ostensibly the reason for welfare cutbacks, here dependency is presented as the *result* of capital and state divestment—Precious and her communities are forced to rely on municipal systems unwilling and unable to support them.

In its articulation of counternarratives of dependency, Sapphire's novel highlights the third function of a crip-of-color critique: an epistemological project. Indeed, a crip-of-color critique highlights not only the ableist reasoning propping up welfare reform but also the "ruptural possibilities" engendered through minority cultural and literary expression that call forth other modes of knowing.[37] In works like *Push*, dependency is reenvisioned as a site of aesthetic and political potentiality, contesting the fictions of state parasitism authored by Reagan and others.[38] The alternative classroom space of Each One Teach One, for instance, offers Precious an informal support network consisting of other young women of color who depend on one another for joy and survival and who honor one another's vulnerabilities. And while Ms. Rain's classroom cannot compensate for the intensifying resource disparities of Reagan-era New York City, it at least envisions an infrastructural network and ideology of care that intervenes into the calculus of life value determined by welfare reform, insisting on the inherent worth of Black, brown, poor, queer, and disabled lives. Literary and cultural production—particularly by women of color and queers of color—thus constitutes a vital site of knowledge and theorization in crip-of-color critique's conceptual armature.

Yet, rather than taking a uniformly optimistic view, a crip-of-color critique also recognizes that minority literatures and cultures are not inherently liberatory and can also operate in service of disciplinary norms. The hyperbolic depiction of the welfare queen in *Push*, for instance, potentially reaffirms dominant welfare mythology even as it simultaneously condemns the deadly logics of reform. Further, the literacy bildungsroman as genre mirrors in many ways the curative narratives of antiwelfare policy, which similarly imagined welfare recipients as part of a developmental trajectory and as pitiable subjects in need of redemption. Given these limitations, while *Push* does partially illustrate the aims of crip-of-color critique, this framework is more fully realized in Ward's *Salvage the Bones*.

"Everything Deserve to Live": Mothering Interdependency in *Salvage the Bones*

Akin to my reading of *Push*, Ward's *Salvage* foregrounds how storylines of dependent subjectivity, articulated through its reimagining of the welfare mother, can interrupt the logic of disposability that casts racialized and disabled populations as parasitic, unproductive, and without value. Ward's novel suggests that a politics and aesthetics of dependency are not just possible but necessary for the survival of those populations cast as drains on the state. In this way, *Salvage* furthers a key value of feminist disability scholarship, which has long highlighted the "nested dependencies" that enable collective life.[39] In the disabling context of infrastructural erosion, *Salvage the Bones* posits interdependency as a primary means of mothering a viable world. Here, survival hinges not on the achievement of independence but on the recognition and cultivation of the support networks that enable the characters to endure.

Published fifteen years after the passage of major US welfare reform, Ward's *Salvage the Bones* centrally contends with the punishing legacies and structuring presence of state infrastructural abandonment. Ward's novel unfolds in the fictional Mississippi Gulf town of Bois Sauvage, documenting the impoverished Batiste family in both their maintenance of everyday life and their preparations for imminent emergency. The emergency in question is Hurricane Katrina, a disaster intensified through a spectacular failure of public infrastructure: the failure of levees, emergency prevention, and federal assistance. As the data show, $71 million evaporated from the budget of the US Army Corps of Engineers in 2005, denying necessary improvements to the city's levee system.[40] Local, state, and federal emergency response systems collapsed in Katrina's wake, both unprepared for and unwilling to navigate a disaster of such unprecedented scale. And while the connection to the 1996 Personal Responsibility and Work Opportunity Reconciliation Act may initially seem scant, Katrina's horrific repercussions, as many have noted, were the culmination of years of assaults on public infrastructural upkeep. "Soon after Hurricane Katrina hit the Gulf Coast," wrote educational scholar Henry Giroux, "the consequences of the long legacy of attacking big government and bleeding the social and public sectors of the state became glaringly evident."[41] The aftermath of the storm is, in many ways, the outcome of welfare reform's deadly ideologies.

While New Orleans was the primary backdrop for this drama of state abandonment, Ward's Bois Sauvage, too, is indelibly shaped by the erosion of public services. There is the hospital, mentioned repeatedly throughout the novel, that none of the Batistes want to visit; it remains inaccessible for reasons we can only infer. There is the lone phone call from the state government, issued by a man with an "iron throat," that mandates evacuation using the language of personal responsibility: "If you choose to stay in your home and have not evacuated by this time, we are not responsible. . . . These are the consequences of your actions."[42] And there is the "birth in a bare-bulb place," the title of the first chapter, which refers to both the Batiste homestead, named the Pit, and the work of birthing and mothering that is the novel's narrative engine. While the Batiste family cobbles together some semblance of protection against the storm, the protagonist, fifteen-year-old Esch Batiste, grapples with the knowledge of her unexpected pregnancy. And though *Salvage the Bones* does not engage explicitly with the welfare mother stereotype, it nonetheless centralizes the figure of the Black teen mother, who, according to Ward herself, "continues to loom large in the public consciousness" and provides a mythology of mothering that is "still too useful to some."[43]

Salvage the Bones, in all its mythic preoccupation with mothering, suggests that we need new narratives of racialized mothering to navigate an era wrought by infrastructural erosion, in which the most basic structures for sustaining life have quite literally been washed away. Yet, rather than asking the Black women and mothers buried beneath these state-sanctioned myths to "come clean," to borrow Hortense Spillers's formulation,[44] Ward's novel instead counters myth with myth, redirecting myth's social and often sacred function to produce new systems of thought for a culture bent on punishing its most vulnerable members. In the face of state brutality, *Salvage the Bones* offers countermythologies of mothering in which interdependence constitutes the infrastructure necessary to contest systemic neglect.

Resonant with the 2016 anthology *Revolutionary Mothering: Love on the Front Lines*, originally titled *This Bridge Called My Baby*,[45] in *Salvage the Bones* mothering functions not as biological imperative or property relation but as a repertoire of what Gumbs terms "transformative bridge-making acts."[46] This description enables us to see mothering as a kind of infrastructural labor: the practice of "creating, nurturing, affirming," and above all, "supporting" life.[47] Returning to the infrastructural hermeneutic of crip-of-color critique, I view the bridge of these "bridge-making acts," as well as the bridge of the original *This Bridge Called My Back*,[48] as not just metaphors but infrastructural figures that speak to the crises of state support unfolding in Reagan's wake. Intervening into the social order reproduced by the welfare queen myth, which leveraged the specter of dependency to argue that some people deserve less than others, *Salvage the Bones* instead mothers a vision of survival that encompasses all forms of life. As sixteen-year-old Skeetah Batiste puts it, "Everything deserve to live."[49]

This vision of survival importantly unfolds as a crip or disability ethos, as it contests the consequences of an ideology of ability while suggesting interdependency as a primary mode of survival. Erica R. Edwards describes the novel's ethical code as such: "Here, the weak survive, and survival articulates itself as the preservation of collectivity against singularity."[50] Similarly, Annie Bares draws on disability theory to identify the novel's "rejection of pity or compassion as organizing principles for relationships among characters" in favor of "relationships based on an acknowledgement of mutual dependence."[51] Building on Edwards's and Bares's insights, I describe this ethos as *crip* because it takes bodily vulnerability as a given, approaching physical and psychological needs as simple matters of fact rather than evidence of pathology. As disability justice activist Patricia Berne put it, "All bodies have strengths and needs that must be met," and following this, we must "attempt to meet each other's needs as we build toward liberation."[52] Through its ethos of interdependency, or the "preservation of collectivity against singularity," *Salvage the Bones* furthers a crip vision of reciprocity, sketching out an alternate social order in which vulnerable human and nonhuman lives mutually enable one another.[53] Drawing on the world-making properties of myth, it describes what can or even must arise in the context of state neglect.

This alternate order begins with a myth of creation: the birth in a bare-bulb place. Accordingly, *Salvage*'s chapter structure and titling conventions mimic the Book of Genesis; its plot is spaced out over twelve days, each corresponding with a chapter title: "The First Day," "The Second Day," and so forth. And for all its unrelenting realism, the novel nonetheless signals its adoption of mythic structures as a means of imagining a habitable world. For instance, Esch Batiste calls on the myth of Medea, vengeful mother and sorceress, to give narrative form and meaning to her own conundrum of creation: "My stomach sizzles sickly, so I pull my book from the corner of my bed where it's smashed between the wall and my mattress. In *Mythology*, I am still reading about Medea and the quest for the Golden Fleece. Here is someone I recognize . . . I know her."[54] Upon Medea's ancient stage, Esch plays out the events of her own life, a practice that is a primary means of psychic survival.

Myths, according to Patricia Yaeger, function as this kind of social blueprint, as they "establish long-term models for guiding behavior."[55] They require, first, mystery; second, a topos, or "an explication of cosmic shape"; third, an epistemology; and fourth, an "ethic—a set of rules or maxims about how to live within the parameters of the everyday."[56] The birth in a bare-bulb place, then, outlines the cosmic shape of the world that the Batistes both inhabit and endure. The Pit, as Esch describes it, is the bare-bulb place, which refers both to its primary source of light— the bare bulb—and to the bare essentials of formal support and power to which the Batistes have access. The birth references two separate but interconnected events: the past memory of Esch's mother dying in childbirth, illuminated by the bare bulb, and the present event of China, Skeetah Batiste's prized pit bull, giving birth to puppies. It also foreshadows the anticipated birth of Esch's child, which she carries in secret.

Like *Push*, the birth in a bare-bulb place entangles infrastructural violence with the phantom of deviant mothering, layering the self-obliterating labor of giving life with the grid of electric power: "Mama had all of us in her bed, under her own bare burning bulb, so when it was time for Junior, she thought she could do the same. It didn't work out that way."[57] The bulb also figures into China's own violent experience with birthing: "What China is doing is fighting, like she was born to do. Fight our shoes, fight other dogs, fight these puppies that are reaching for the outside, blind and wet. . . . It's quiet. Heavy. Feels like it should be raining, but it isn't. There are no stars, and the bare bulbs of the Pit burn."[58] This scene of birth twinned with death, of worlds both made and unmade, reformats another iconic scene of power and creation: the subterranean light installation that bookends Ralph Ellison's novel *Invisible Man* (1952). Viewing himself as part of "the great American tradition of tinkers," which include Thomas Edison and Benjamin Franklin, Ellison's protagonist famously gives life to "1,369" light bulbs powered by stolen electricity.[59] His seizing of the grid is not a purely aesthetic move but, rather, signifies an attempt to effect social change. As a tinker and inventor, the Invisible Man signals the need to create the world anew through the radical redirection of light and power.[60]

In *Salvage the Bones*, the burning bulb similarly draws on electricity's transformative properties. It illuminates another possible horizon for organizing social life, one that redraws the boundaries of the individual self and its claims to bodily wholeness. We see, for instance, how the birthing process both undoes and exceeds the self, transforming the bodies of Mama and of China, the pit bull: "She seems to be turning herself inside out . . . China is blooming."[61] In pregnancy, as Lily Gurton-Wachter has written, "the distinction you once knew between self and other comes undone."[62] Pregnancy, too, describes a system of interdependent relations; the fetus and the pregnant person are linked, if only temporarily, in their bids for survival. And while pregnancy and disability are not one and the same, they nonetheless both name categories of being that highlight the inherent changeability and porosity of bodies, thus aligning this origin myth with the novel's crip ethos. "Disability," according to feminist disability scholar Rosemarie Garland-Thomson, "invites us to query what the continuity of the self might depend upon if the body perpetually metamorphoses" and, in so doing, critiques the "normalizing phallic fantasies of wholeness, unity, coherence, and completeness."[63] Akin to disability activism and theory, the myth of the burning bulb takes the vulnerable, fractured, and changeable body as a given, placing it at the center of the novel's alternate social order. In this way, the burning-bulb narrative demonstrates the world-making properties of dependency and vulnerability, insofar as it describes a cosmos generated from, rather than despite, embodied fragility.

The opening scene further undoes the differential worth assigned to human and nonhuman subjects, as it throws into question the hierarchies of life that value some forms of existence above others. This becomes evident in the mirroring language used to describe China and Mama Batiste, which, rather than reducing Mama to the status of animal, underscores the connection between two beings whose reproduction is similarly framed as a societal threat. And animals, rather than occupying a lesser or subordinate position, coexist with their human companions in a mutual interrelation of need. "Some people," Skeetah Batiste observes, "understand that between man and dog is a relationship. Equal."[64] Though *Salvage the Bones* articulates this vision of interspecies reciprocity throughout its pages, the opening scene sets the stage for this ethos of interdependence, as it highlights the all-encompassing love between Skeetah Batiste, Esch's older brother, and China, his pit bull. Waiting for China to give birth, Skeetah sleeps with her nightly in the shed, "curled around China like a fingernail around flesh."[65] And just as China provides Skeetah with saleable puppies and companionship, so Skeetah devotes himself to their survival in a world bent on their undoing: "They're going to live, and they're going to be big."[66] Rather than making appeals to self-ownership and independence, then, the novel's bare bulb sheds light on a world in which human and nonhuman life form an informal structure of support, generating an interspecies network of assistance in which the most vulnerable life-forms might (yet often do not) endure.

And then there is the bare bulb itself, which as a recurring image of power and provision sketches its own mythology of mothering, survival, and creation. At its most surface level, the bare bulb signals the poverty of the Batiste family, who get by largely through the work of salvaging: auto parts, wood scraps, flooring, and so forth. It also depicts, with swiftness and economy, the regime of resource deprivation that intensified Katrina's destruction. Yet the bulb signals more than just infrastructural violence; it also accompanies, again and again, the acts and figures of deviant mothering on which the novel turns. *Salvage the Bones* describes China, one of the novel's many mothers, as "burning bright," "so bright it is hard to look at her."[67] Like the bare bulb, China is fragile and vulnerable yet in all of her vulnerability exudes a paradoxical kind of power. When Manny, Esch's romantic interest, suggests to Skeetah that China, as recent mother, is too weak to fight, Skeetah replies: "You serious? That's when they come into they strength. They got something to protect. . . . That's power. . . . To give life . . . is to know what's worth fighting for."[68] The bare bulb and China both convey a myth of mothering in which power paradoxically hinges on fragility. Both can burn so brightly only *because* of their fragility, thus remapping the terrain of what power is or can be. Mothering, then, also taps into the epistemic registers of myth—that is, mothering as a means of knowing power differently, and as a system of thought that frames seemingly expendable life as "worth fighting for."[69]

But the labor of mothering a habitable world, as *Salvage the Bones* suggests, must go beyond a myth of creation. It also requires a myth of destruction, or of unmaking a world incompatible with Black life. Enter Hurricane Katrina, recast in Ward's imagination as "the mother who swept into the Gulf and slaughtered."[70] For many of us, Katrina is synonymous with slaughter, a force that dealt death along raced and classed lines. But when readers come to know Katrina as *mother*, a word that also signals the work of transformation, she becomes Oya, the Yoruban goddess of storms, winds, and change. According to Luisah Teish, one of the original contributors to *This Bridge Called My Back*, Oya "brings sudden structural change in people and things. [She] does not just rearrange the furniture in the house—she knocks the building to the ground and blows away the floor tiles."[71] And so, while Katrina makes short work of the Batiste homestead, she also washes away the "yacht club, and all the white-columned homes that faced the beach, that made us feel small and dirty and poorer than ever."[72] She destroys the material emblems of a social system that reproduces poverty for families like the Batistes. Both types of property, once unequal in value, are now leveled and wiped clean, a necessary prerequisite for mothering something altogether new.

Katrina, in all her destruction, nonetheless generates a possible future for the residents of Bois Sauvage. Significantly, she spares the Batistes and their neighboring friends and family. In Ward's imaginary, she is "the murderous mother who cut us to the bone but left us alive. . . . She left us to learn to crawl. She left us to salvage."[73] Katrina as mythic mother thus promotes a vision of survival above all: the final chapter, in which Katrina retreats, bears the title "Alive." What's more, she gestures toward the survival of Black and economically distressed communities abandoned by the state. In this way, Ward's novel reverses a dominant narrative of Katrina that transformed the survivors of the hurricane into looters and criminals through rhetorics of personal responsibility. By framing the residents of Bois Sauvage as survivors, and by generating myths that can mother survival, *Salvage the Bones* intervenes into a calculus of life value that insists on the expendability of some in order to support the rest. It generates the possibility of a world in which hierarchies of life no longer hold traction, whether determined by race, ability, or species.

This vision of survival, articulated through a countermythology of mothering, is pointedly not survival of the fittest (as in those with economic, racial, and able-bodied privilege) but survival of the most vulnerable. In the Pit, the vulnerable are left alive, and survival is the product of mutual support and reciprocity rather than of self-preservation. The novel thus conceptualizes survival as an insistence on care as a collective project that emerges through the interlocking efforts of many dependent life-forms. This is a vision contingent on the interdependence of beings, one that honors the infrastructures of care and support cultivated in Bois Sauvage.

This vision of survival is perhaps most fully articulated in the closing scene. The storm has receded, and Skeetah has begun his search for China, who was carried away by Katrina—the devouring of one mother by another. Esch's language shifts into the future tense:

> We will sit with [Skeetah] here . . . We will sit until we are sleepy . . . until Junior falls asleep in Randall's arms, his weak neck lolling off Randall's elbow. Randall will watch Junior and Big Henry will watch me and I will watch Skeetah, and Skeetah will watch none of us . . . He will look into the future and see her emerge into the circle of his fire. . . . dull but alive, alive, alive [. . .] *China*. She will return. . . . She will know that I have kept watch, that I have fought. China will bark and call me sister . . . She will know that I am a mother.[74]

Here, Ward describes a vision of China's return that can manifest only through the collective efforts of the Batiste siblings and their friend Big

Henry. This manifestation of *will*, the operative term of the future tense, assumes the form of a human chain, an infrastructural network of support that links bodies and futures together. Esch's usage of the future tense, a means of "willing" China back into the world, intervenes into narratives of expendability to insist on the survival of racialized, disabled, and impoverished populations. Her usage of *will* is a mode of production toward a social world that does not yet exist, a world in which China is written back into existence and recognizes Esch as a mother. Here arises the final myth of mothering, a myth in which one becomes a mother through the labor of keeping watch, of fighting, of surviving, a myth in which one is not born but becomes a mother through infrastructural labor, which can build a bridge from the ruins of Bois Sauvage to another mode of social life. This is, above all, a myth of radical mothering that insists on the recuperation of dependency and the recognition of shared vulnerability as a primary mode of survival and as a means of generating a possible future for lives that survive against all odds: "*Tomorrow*," Esch thinks, "*everything will be washed clean.* What I carry in my stomach is relentless; like each unbearable day, it will dawn."[75]

Conclusion

The crip ethos and vision derived from Ward's *Salvage the Bones* encapsulate, in many ways, the framework I have termed crip-of-color critique. *Salvage* articulates a system of values that (a) honors the vulnerability and dependency of living creatures, as well as their differing needs for support; (b) divests from the hierarchies of race, species, and ability underlying the uneven distribution of resources; (c) underscores the disabling brutality of state divestment; and (d) envisions alternate modes of sociality organized around care for other living beings, regardless of blood relation or similarity to the self. And while disability haunts Ward's novel with its scenes of scarring, mutilation, sickness, and dismemberment, a crip-of-color critique is less interested in disability as a set of identifiable diagnoses and more invested in disability as an analytic for thinking across landscapes of racialized state neglect.

A crip-of-color critique thus demonstrates the utility of a disability politic in overturning the punitive ideologies of welfare reform. It not only foregrounds the ableism undergirding state discourses of dependency but also challenges and overwrites these dominant narratives. Under the terms of this framework, the recuperation of dependency emerges as a key political project, a tactic that upholds the survival against all odds of a "disruptive vulnerability that refuses to disappear."[76] Further, in taking dependency as a given, a crip-of-color critique offers an infrastructural hermeneutic that reads for relations of support, whether social, material, or prosthetic. Yet, rather than uncritically celebrating infrastructure, this framework also attends to the asymmetries of support relations, paying attention to how white supremacy, heteropatriarchy, ableism, and capitalism determine uneven economies of resource provision. Finally, a crip-of-color critique also recognizes the limitations inherent in a utopian discourse of interdependence that, in highlighting networks of informal care, potentially further erodes state accountability by suggesting that vulnerable populations can and should support themselves. Even in *Push* and *Salvage*, the informal networks that arise in the absence of infrastructure are still not enough: Precious may gain literacy and Esch may survive the storm, but their futures nonetheless remain circumscribed by material deprivation. And so, while a crip-of-color critique explores the political potential of interdependence, it does not frame this value as a cure-all for contemporary crises of care.

Given the association of racial and gendered deviance with state parasitism and the subsequent erosion of social safety nets, a crip-of-color critique argues for the reconsideration of dependency as a crucial step toward addressing disabling structures of state neglect. And in cripping the welfare queen, it forges an alliance among antiracist, anticapitalist, and feminist disability politics, one modeled, if imperfectly, by the relationship between Precious and her baby daughter, Little Mongo. In this way, a crip-of-color critique speaks to the "radical potential" outlined in "Punks, Bulldaggers, and Welfare Queens," through which Cathy Cohen envisions a politics in which "one's relation to power, and not some homogenized identity, is privileged in determining one's political comrades."[77] Only by recognizing the links between the marginalization of welfare queens and their disabled kin can we develop critical analytics that can "[confront] the linked yet varied sites of power in this country."[78]

Jina B. Kim is assistant professor of English and the study of women and gender at Smith College. She is currently writing a manuscript titled *Dreaming of Infrastructure: Crip-of-Color Imaginaries after the US Welfare State.* Her essays have appeared in *Signs, American Quarterly, MELUS,* and the *Asian American Literary Review.*

Notes

1. Cohen, "Punks, Bulldaggers, and Welfare Queens," 438. In addition to Cohen's article, some key examples of feminist scholarship intervening into antiwelfare discourses of Black mothering include Dorothy Roberts, *Killing the Black Body*; Hortense Spillers, "Mama's Baby, Papa's Maybe"; Collins, *Black Feminist Thought*; Hancock, *Politics of Disgust*; and Lubiano, "Black Ladies, Welfare Queens, and State Minstrels."
2. Cohen, "Punks, Bulldaggers, and Welfare Queens," 438.
3. Sapphire, *Push*, 34.

4. Michelle Jarman first noted the connection between Sapphire's *Push* and disability politics in "Cultural Consumption and Rejection of Precious Jones."

5. Ferguson, *Aberrations in Black*, 26.

6. Lubiano, "Black Ladies, Welfare Queens, and State Minstrels," 331.

7. Schram, *After Welfare*, 59.

8. Gumbs, "We Can Learn to Mother Ourselves," 206. See also Singer, *Erotic Wellfare*.

9. Gumbs, "We Can Learn to Mother Ourselves," 207.

10. Cohen, "Punks, Bulldaggers, and Welfare Queens," 440.

11. Berne, "Disability Justice."

12. While my focus here is on welfare reform and state divestment, other scholars have analyzed the centrality of ableist logic to other forms of state violence, such as police brutality, the prison-industrial complex, and public education. For more on disability and the prison-industrial complex, see Ben-Moshe, Chapman, and Carey, *Disability Incarcerated*; Ben-Moshe, *Decarcerating Disability*. For more on disability and police brutality, see Ritchie, *Invisible No More*, chap. 4. For more on disability and US public education, see Erevelles, "Educating Unruly Bodies"; and Annamma, *Pedagogy of Pathologization*.

13. Sandahl, "Queering the Crip or Cripping the Queer?," 37.

14. Minich, "Enabling Whom?"

15. Fraser and Gordon, "Genealogy of Dependency," 332.

16. Clare, *Brilliant Imperfection*, 145.

17. For examples of disability justice discussions of interdependence, see Clare, *Brilliant Imperfection*; Piepzna-Samarasinha, *Care Work*; Berne et al., "Ten Principles of Disability Justice"; and Mingus, "Interdependency."

18. Mingus, "Interdependency."

19. Hong and Ferguson, introduction, 1–2.

20. Hong and Ferguson, introduction, 2.

21. Frye, *Birthing Disability*, 100.

22. Davidson, "Universal Design," 118.

23. See Spade, *Normal Life*.

24. See Bagenstos, "Americans with Disabilities Act as Welfare Reform."

25. Puar, "Coda," 154.

26. Jarman, "Cultural Consumption and Rejection of Precious Jones," 164.

27. Abdur-Rahman, *Against the Closet*, 133.

28. Yaeger, "Introduction," 15.

29. Rubenstein, Robbins, and Beal, "Infrastructuralism," 576.

30. Jackson, *Social Works*, 8; Jackson, "Working Publics," 10.

31. Sapphire, *Push*, 1.

32. Abdur-Rahman, *Against the Closet*, 133.

33. Frye, *Birthing Disability*, 100.

34. Sapphire, *Push*, 132.

35. James and Wu, "Editors' Introduction," 4.

36. In addition to Moynihan's infamous 1965 report, the work of antiwelfare pundits Charles Murray and Lawrence Mead also forwards cultural/behavioral explanations for racialized poverty. See Murray, *Losing Ground*; Mead, *The New Politics of Poverty*.

37. Ferguson, *Aberrations in Black*, 26.

38. For more on the discourse of dependency in pre- and postindustrial contexts, see Fraser and Gordon, "Genealogy of Dependency."

39. Kittay, *Love's Labor*, 141.
40. See Sanyika, "Katrina and the Condition of Black New Orleans."
41. Giroux, "Reading Hurricane Katrina," 174.
42. Ward, *Salvage the Bones*, 217.
43. Ward, *Salvage the Bones*, 265.
44. Spillers, "Mama's Baby, Papa's Maybe," 65.
45. Gumbs, Martens, and Williams, *Revolutionary Mothering*.
46. Gumbs, introduction, 9.
47. Gumbs, introduction, 9.
48. Moraga and Anzaldúa, *This Bridge Called My Back*.
49. Ward, *Salvage the Bones*, 213.
50. Edwards, "Sex after the Black Normal,"158.
51. Bares, "'Each Unbearable Day,'" 32.
52. Berne, "Disability Justice"; Berne et al., "Ten Principles of Disability Justice," 228.
53. Edwards, "Sex after the Black Normal," 158.
54. Ward, *Salvage the Bones*, 38.
55. Yaeger, *"Beasts of the Southern Wild."*
56. Yaeger, *"Beasts of the Southern Wild."*
57. Ward, *Salvage the Bones*, 2.
58. Ward, *Salvage the Bones*, 2.
59. Ellison, *Invisible Man*, 7.
60. For more on the trope of electricity in *Invisible Man*, see Ford, "Crossroads and Cross-Currents in *Invisible Man*."
61. Ward, *Salvage the Bones*, 4.
62. Gurton-Wachter, "Stranger Guest."
63. Garland-Thomson, "Integrating Disability," 20, 28.
64. Ward, *Salvage the Bones*, 29.
65. Ward, *Salvage the Bones*, 3.
66. Ward, *Salvage the Bones*, 21.
67. Ward, *Salvage the Bones*, 103, 168.
68. Ward, *Salvage the Bones*, 96.
69. Ward, *Salvage the Bones*, 96.
70. Ward, *Salvage the Bones*, 255.
71. Teish, *Jambalaya*, 120.
72. Ward, *Salvage the Bones*, 252.
73. Ward, *Salvage the Bones*, 255.
74. Ward, *Salvage the Bones*, 258.
75. Ward, *Salvage the Bones*, 205.
76. Erevelles, "Thinking with Disability Studies."
77. Cohen, "Punks, Bulldaggers, and Welfare Queens," 438.
78. Cohen, "Punks, Bulldaggers, and Welfare Queens," 462.

References

Abdur-Rahman, Aliyyah. *Against the Closet: Black Political Longing and the Erotics of Race*. Durham, NC: Duke University Press, 2012.
Annamma, Subini Ancy. *The Pedagogy of Pathologization: Dis/abled Girls of Color in the School-Prison Nexus*. New York: Routledge, 2018.
Bagenstos, Samuel. "The Americans with Disabilities Act as Welfare Reform." *William and Mary Law Review* 44, no. 3 (2003): 921–1027.

Ben-Moshe, Liat. *Decarcerating Disability: Deinstitutionalization and Prison Abolition.* Minneapolis: University of Minnesota Press, 2020.

Ben-Moshe, Liat, Chris Chapman, and Allison C. Carey, eds. *Disability Incarcerated: Imprisonment and Disability in the United States and Canada.* New York: Palgrave Macmillan, 2014.

Bares, Annie. "'Each Unbearable Day': Narrative Ruthlessness and Environmental and Reproductive Injustice in Jesmyn Ward's *Salvage the Bones.*" *MELUS* 44, no. 3 (2019): 21–40.

Berne, Patricia. "Disability Justice—A Working Draft." *Sins Invalid: An Unashamed Claim to Beauty in the Face of Invisibility,* June 9, 2015. www.sinsinvalid.org/blog /disability-justice-a-working-draft-by-patty-berne.

Berne, Patricia, Aurora Levins Morales, David Langstaff, and Sins Invalid. "Ten Principles of Disability Justice." *WSQ* 46, nos. 1–2 (2018): 227–30.

Clare, Eli. *Brilliant Imperfection: Grappling with Cure.* Durham, NC: Duke University Press, 2017.

Cohen, Cathy. "Punks, Bulldaggers, and Welfare Queens: The Radical Potential of Queer Politics?" *GLQ* 3, no. 4 (1997): 437–65.

Collins, Patricia Hill. *Black Feminist Thought: Knowledge, Consciousness, and the Politics of Empowerment.* Boston: Unwin Hyman, 1990.

Davidson, Michael. "Universal Design: The Work of Disability in an Age of Globalization." In *The Disability Studies Reader,* 2nd ed., edited by Lennard Davis, 117–28. New York: Routledge, 2006.

Edwards, Erica R. "Sex after the Black Normal." *differences* 26, no. 1 (2015): 141–67.

Ellison, Ralph. *Invisible Man.* 1952; repr., New York: Random House, 1995.

Erevelles, Nirmala. "Educating Unruly Bodies: Critical Pedagogy, Disability Studies, and the Politics of Schooling." *Educational Theory* 50, no. 1 (2000): 25–47.

Erevelles, Nirmala. "Thinking with Disability Studies." *Disability Studies Quarterly* 34, no. 2 (2014). doi.org/10.18061/dsq.v34i2.4248.

Ferguson, Roderick A. *Aberrations in Black: Toward a Queer of Color Critique.* Minneapolis: University of Minnesota Press, 2003.

Ford, Douglas. "Crossroads and Cross-currents in *Invisible Man.*" *MFS: Modern Fiction Studies* 45, no. 4 (1999): 887–904.

Fraser, Nancy, and Linda Gordon. "A Genealogy of Dependency: Tracing a Keyword of the U.S. Welfare State." *Signs* 19, no. 2 (1994): 309–36.

Frye, Lezlie. "Birthing Disability, Reproducing Race: Uneasy Intersections in Post– Civil Rights Politics of U.S. Citizenship." PhD diss., New York University, 2016.

Garland-Thomson, Rosemarie. "Integrating Disability, Transforming Feminist Theory." *NWSA Journal* 14, no. 3 (2002): 1–32.

Giroux, Henry. "Reading Hurricane Katrina: Race, Class, and the Biopolitics of Disposability." *College Literature* 3, no. 3 (2006): 171–96.

Gumbs, Alexis Pauline. Introduction to Gumbs, Martens, and Williams, *Revolutionary Mothering,* 9–10.

Gumbs, Alexis Pauline. "'We Can Learn to Mother Ourselves': The Queer Survival of Black Feminism 1968–1996." PhD diss., Duke University, 2010.

Gumbs, Alexis Pauline, China Martens, and Mai'a Williams, eds. *Revolutionary Mothering: Love on the Front Lines.* Oakland, CA: PM Press, 2016.

Gurton-Wachter, Lily. "The Stranger Guest: The Literature of Pregnancy and New Motherhood." *Los Angeles Review of Books,* July 27, 2016. lareviewofbooks.org /article/stranger-guest-literature-pregnancy-new-motherhood/.

Hancock, Ange-Marie. *The Politics of Disgust: The Public Identity of the Welfare Queen.* New York: New York University Press, 2004.

Hong, Grace Kyungwon, and Roderick A. Ferguson. Introduction to *Strange Affinities: The Gender and Sexual Politics of Comparative Racialization*, edited by Grace Kyungwon Hong and Roderick A. Ferguson, 1–24. Durham, NC: Duke University Press, 2011.

Jackson, Shannon. *Social Works: Performing Art, Supporting Publics*. New York: Routledge, 2011.

Jackson, Shannon. "Working Publics." *Performance Research* 16, no. 2 (2011): 8–13.

James, Jennifer C., and Cynthia Wu. "Editors' Introduction: Race, Ethnicity, Disability, and Literature: Intersections and Interventions." *MELUS* 31, no. 3 (2006): 3–13.

Jarman, Michelle. "Cultural Consumption and Rejection of Precious Jones: Pushing Disability in to the Discussion of Sapphire's *Push* and Lee Daniels's *Precious*." *Feminist Formations* 24, no. 2 (2012): 162–85.

Kittay, Eva Feder. *Love's Labor: Essays on Women, Equality, and Dependency*. New York: Routledge, 1998.

Lubiano, Wahneema. "Black Ladies, Welfare Queens, and State Minstrels: Ideological War by Narrative Means." In *Race-ing Justice, En-gendering Power: Essays on Anita Hill, Clarence Thomas, and the Construction of Social Reality*, edited by Toni Morrison, 323–63. New York: Pantheon, 1992.

Mead, Lawrence. *The New Politics of Poverty: The Nonworking Poor in America*. New York: Basic Books, 1992.

Mingus, Mia. "Interdependency (Excerpts from Several Talks)." *Leaving Evidence*, January 22, 2010. leavingevidence.wordpress.com/2010/01/22/interdependency-exerpts-from-several-talks/.

Minich, Julie Avril. "Enabling Whom? Critical Disability Studies Now." *Lateral* 5, no. 1 (2016). doi.org/10.25158/L5.1.9.

Moraga, Cherríe L., and Gloria E. Anzaldúa. *This Bridge Called My Back: Writings by Radical Women of Color*. Watertown, MA: Persephone, 1981.

Murray, Charles. *Losing Ground: American Social Policy 1950–1980*. New York: Basic Books, 1984.

Piepzna-Samarasinha, Leah Lakshmi. *Care Work: Dreaming Disability Justice*. Vancouver, BC: Arsenal Pulp, 2018.

Puar, Jasbir. "Coda: The Cost of Getting Better: Suicide, Sensation, Switchpoints." *GLQ* 18, no. 1 (2011): 147–58.

Ritchie, Andrea. *Invisible No More: Police Violence against Black Women and Women of Color*. Boston: Beacon, 2017.

Roberts, Dorothy. *Killing the Black Body: Race, Reproduction, and the Meaning of Liberty*. New York: Pantheon, 1997.

Rubenstein, Michael, Bruce Robbins, and Sophia Beal. "Infrastructuralism: An Introduction." In "Infrastructuralism," edited by Michael Rubenstein, Bruce Robbins, and Sophia Beal. Special issue, *Modern Fiction Studies* 61, no. 4 (2015): 576–85.

Sandahl, Carrie. "Queering the Crip or Cripping the Queer? Intersections of Queer and Crip Identities in Solo Autobiographical Performance." *GLQ* 9, no. 1–2 (2003): 25–56.

Sanyika, Mtangulizi. "Katrina and the Condition of Black New Orleans: The Struggle for Justice, Equity, and Democracy." In *Race, Place, and Environmental Justice after Hurricane Katrina: Struggles to Reclaim, Rebuild, and Revitalize New Orleans and the Gulf Coast*, edited by Robert D. Bullard and Beverly Wright, 153–212. Boulder, CO: Westview, 2009.

Sapphire. *Push*. New York: Knopf, 1996.

Schram, Sanford F. *After Welfare: The Culture of Postindustrial Social Policy*. New York: New York University Press, 2000.

Singer, Linda. *Erotic Welfare: Sexual Theory and Politics in the Age of Epidemic*. New York: Routledge, 1992.

Spade, Dean. *Normal Life: Administrative Violence, Critical Trans Politics, and the Limits of Law*. Cambridge, MA: South End, 2011.

Spillers, Hortense. "Mama's Baby, Papa's Maybe: An American Grammar Book." *Diacritics* 17, no. 2 (1987): 64–81.

Teish, Luisah. *Jambalaya: The Natural Woman's Book of Personal Charms and Practical Rituals*. New York: HarperCollins, 1988.

Ward, Jesmyn. *Salvage the Bones*. New York: Bloomsbury, 2011.

Yaeger, Patricia. "*Beasts of the Southern Wild* and Dirty Ecology." *Southern Spaces*, February 13, 2013. southernspaces.org/2013/beasts-southern-wild-and-dirty-ecology/.

Yaeger, Patricia. "Introduction: Dreaming of Infrastructure." *PMLA* 122, no. 1 (2007): 9–26.